Slavoj Žiž

ONE WEEK LOAN

Also available from Continuum:

Slavoj Žižek: Live Theory

Rex Butler

continuum
NEW YORK • LONDON

Continuum

The Tower Building, 11 York Road, London SE1 7NX

15 East 26th Street, New York, NY 10010

British Library Cataloguing-in-Publication Data
A catalogue record for this book is available from the British Library.

ISBN: HB: 0-8264-6994-9
    PB: 0-8264-6995-7

Library of Congress Cataloging-in-Publication Data
A catalog record for this book is available from the Library of Congress.

Typeset by Aarontype Limited, Easton, Bristol.
Printed and bound in Great Britain by MPG Books Ltd, Bodmin, Cornwall.

Contents

Abbreviations

The following books and essays written or edited by Žižek are indicated by initials:

AF   *The Abyss of Freedom/Ages of the World* (Ann Arbor, MI: University of Michigan Press, 1997)

B   *On Belief* (New York and London: Routledge, 2001)

'BS'   'Between Symbolic Fiction and Fantasmatic Spectre: Towards a Lacanian Theory of Ideology', *Analysis* 5 (1994).

CHU   *Contingency, Hegemony, Universality: Contemporary Dialogues on the Left* (with Judith Butler and Ernesto Laclau) (London: Verso, 2000)

CU   *Cogito and the Unconscious* (Durham, NC: Duke University Press, 1998)

'DB'   'Against the Double Blackmail', *New Left Review* 234 (1999)

DR!   *Welcome to the Desert of the Real!* (London: Verso, 2002)

E!   *Enjoy Your Symptom! Jacques Lacan in Hollywood and Out* (New York and London: Routledge, 1992; 2nd edn, 2002)

FA   *The Fragile Absolute, or, Why is the Christian Legacy Worth Fighting For?* (London: Verso, 2000)

H   *Everything You Always Wanted to Know About Lacan (But Were Afraid to Ask Hitchcock)* (London: Verso, 1992)

HP   *Le Plus Sublime des Hystériques − Hegel passe* (Paris: Point Hors Ligne, 1988)

'HR'   'Human Rights and Its Discontents', Lecture given by Žižek at Olin Auditorium, Bard College, NY (16 November, 1999) (http://www.bard.edu/hrp/zizektranscript.htm)

IR   *The Indivisible Remainder: An Essay on Schelling and Related Matters* (London: Verso, 1996)

K   *The Fright of Real Tears: Krzysztof Kieślowski between Theory and Post-Theory* (London: BFI Publishing, 2001)

The following texts by other authors are also indicated by initials.

Another exemplary case: the hero of Stephen King's *The Shining* is a writer who suffers from writer's block. *The Shining* therefore appears to be a variation on the paradigmatic modernist theme of the impossibility of writing, of telling a story. What accounts for the King touch, however, is the fact that this book is the other side of the true horror: a writer who suffers from an irresistible compulsion to write all the time, without end. Is not this writer King himself, who produces up to three thick novels a year? The trauma at the level of the enunciated content (writer's block) is thus clearly the inversion of a much more horrible trauma, which concerns the subject of enunciation (the endless compulsion to write)

(Slavoj Žižek, *For They Know Not What They Do: Enjoyment as a Political Factor*, 2nd edn)

Chapter 1

The subject of philosophy

The authors of books like this are often reluctant to speak of the private lives of their subjects. After all, what has this to do with their work? How is this to help us understand what they write? Our doubts, however, are soon overcome when we consider the Slovenian cultural analyst Slavoj Žižek. For what can we say about him that he does not already say himself? What secret can we reveal that he has not already turned into the punchline to one of his many well-rehearsed jokes? Which other theorist, for example, would allow themselves the following one-liner to illustrate the psychoanalytic concept of the phallus: 'What is the lightest object in the world? The penis, because it is the only one that can be raised by a mere thought' (*TS*, 382–3)? Who else, in a parody of the anthropologist Claude Lévi-Strauss, would observe:

> In the traditional German lavatory, the hole down which the shit disappears is up front, so that it is first laid out for us to inspect; in the traditional French lavatory, it is in the back, so that the shit is meant to disappear as soon as possible; while the Anglo-Saxon (English and American) lavatory presents a kind of synthesis, with the basin full of water, so that the shit floats in it, visible but not to be inspected? (*PF*, 4)

Or, most famously, would confess that, eating in a Chinese restaurant, his greatest fear is not that he will somehow fall into an orgy with his fellow diners but actually end up sharing a meal with them: 'How many people have entered the way of perdition with some innocent gangbang, which at the time was of no great importance to them, and ended up sharing the main dishes at a Chinese restaurant' (*E!*, ix)? Or would cheerfully admit to a whole range of bad habits: not just the usual 'private repulsive rituals' of smelling one's sweat or picking one's nose (*AF*, 80), but the slightly more social ones of watching pornography

(*PF*, 177–80), engaging in cybersex (*IR*, 191–3) and even reading Colleen McCullough (*LA*, 160)?[1]

Now, Lacanian psychoanalysis will recommend as part of its cure a process of radical *externalization*. It is the idea that we must accept that we are entirely responsible for the situation we find ourselves in; that it is our actions, not the motivations behind them, that define us; that there is no inner core of our being, inaccessible to others. It is what Lacan came to call towards the end of his teaching the *identification with the symptom*, and it meant that we are not to hide the idiosyncrasies and sometimes embarrassing tics and quirks that make us up but acknowledge that they are part of who we are. And this is undoubtedly what Žižek is doing here. But, if we can say this, there is one thing that Žižek does not admit to in that list above – and that is the *very symptom of theory itself*. For it really is the most extraordinary spectacle, seeing Žižek lecture. There he stands, this wildly gesticulating, bear-like man, tugging his beard and shirt, dark circles of sweat growing beneath his armpits, his neatly combed hair growing lank and dishevelled, his eyes staring blindly around the room. He speaks rapidly through a strong Central European accent and a lisp, constantly circling back upon himself to try to make himself clearer, threatening never to stop. We feel he is making the same point over and over, but we cannot quite grasp it, and in order to do so he must take in the entirety of Western philosophy and culture, both high and low: from Schoenberg to sci-fi, from quantum mechanics to the latest Hollywood blockbuster, from now-forgotten figures of eighteenth and nineteenth-century German philosophy to the notoriously obscure writings of the French psychoanalyst Jacques Lacan ... Indeed, Lacan once cruelly quipped of James Joyce that, although what he wrote was almost psychotic in its refusal to fix meaning, this writing was also the only thing that saved him from actual psychosis – and we think the same is true of Žižek as well. Žižek's fellow theorist Judith Butler writes on the back cover of one of his books: 'Slavoj lives to theorize', but we suspect the opposite is true and Žižek theorizes to live. Although, as his public performances and writings attest, his work is endlessly shifting, open-ended, refuses to close itself down or draw conclusions – in a word, is psychotic – it is also only the activity of theorizing that saves him, saves him from the very thing this theorizing brings about.

But, for all of our mockery, seeing Žižek speak takes us back to a possibility only rarely glimpsed since the origins of Western civilization. For he reminds us as much as anyone of the ancient Greek heroine Antigone, who insists beyond all reason and ends up sacrificing herself for a tragic cause. That is, we seem to have here a man who is, in the words of Lacan, 'between two deaths' (*S7*, 270), his outer being reduced to a mere shell or remainder. And yet he is also a man who, like Antigone, appears infused by some unstoppable power, possessed by some extraordinary cause in a world that lacks causes.[2] We might say that Žižek is filled with a kind of *death-drive*, a desire for self-extermination, except that what he reveals is that life itself, life in its profoundest sense, is not possible before this going-towards-death; that what we think we sacrifice when we live life like him only has value when seen from the other side. As Lacan says in his Seminar *The Ethics of Psychoanalysis*, in which he discusses Antigone's case, from this other side we can see and live life 'in the form of something already lost' (*S7*, 280). And perhaps even beyond Antigone – who, after all, still did believe in something, still did have a cause – what are we to make of Žižek, who constantly changes his position and ultimately believes in nothing except the 'inherent correctness of theory itself' (*CU*, i)? What would it mean to sacrifice ourselves and everything we believed in (even our cause) for this 'nothing'? And why would we nevertheless go ahead and do it? Is this death the very life of theory, Theory itself as Cause?

The life of theory

Žižek first announced himself to the English-speaking world in 1989 with the publication of *The Sublime Object of Ideology*. It is an at-the-time unexpected fusion of Marx's notion of the commodity, Althusser's concept of interpellation and Lacan's idea of the split subject, in order to elaborate what we might call the *social symptom*. This symptom is for Žižek a way of bringing together – a long-running problem for progressive politics – the specifics of individual psychology with a wider analysis of the social. The fundamental insight of the book – adapted from Ernesto Laclau and Chantal Mouffe's ground-breaking *Hegemony and Socialist Strategy* (1985)[3] – is that the social is essentially divided, antagonistic, unable to be given closure. This has the consequence that the various terms that are used to understand and construct it are themselves provisional, contingent, continually fought over. Thus a term like 'democracy', which is constantly invoked as a desirable goal of society, is not ideologically neutral or unquestionably positive, but the subject of various groups attempting to claim it (*SO*, 98). Each of these attempts necessarily fails, because no one signifier can speak for the entirety of the social; but each group looks for an explanation of this failure to some external and intrusive element, whose removal would restore an imagined wholeness. It is this element that Žižek calls the 'sublime object of ideology': that ambiguous symptom-element that is 'heterogeneous to any given ideological field and at the same time necessary for that field to achieve its closure' (*SO*, 21).

Žižek follows this up two years later with *For They Know Not What They Do: Enjoyment as a Political Factor*. This densely theoretical text – as if to underscore its political relevance – was originally delivered as a series of two-part lectures over the winter of 1989–90 to a general audience in the months leading up to the first free Slovenian elections after the fall of communism. These were elections in which Žižek himself stood as a pro-reform candidate for the Liberal Democratic Party. *For They Know Not* is, in part at least, a continuation of the enquiry into that fantasmatic 'sublime object', typically a Jew or foreigner, that allows the social to constitute itself as a whole. As Žižek writes in the Introduction, in his typical manner of making a serious point with a joke, if in *Sublime Object* he was able to count on the humour of the Jewish man who, wishing to emigrate from Russia and giving as one of his reasons his fear of anti-Semitic violence with the rise of the new nationalisms and being told that there is nothing to worry about because communism will last forever, was able to reply: 'Well, that is my second reason!', this is no longer the case (*TK*, 1). Today, it is precisely the upsurge of racist violence with the collapse of communism that is the reason for the Jewish man wanting to leave. And here Žižek speaks of the way that, along with the apparently non-ideological 'enjoyment' that allows ideology, there is also underlying this racism the fear of the theft of our enjoyment by others, the resentment of foreign invaders who threaten our way of life because of the strange new ways they have of enjoying themselves (*TK*, 37–8, 213–14).

The innovative aspect of both of these books is the way they are able to revive the traditional category of ideology-critique in these supposedly 'post-ideological' times. Indeed, they are able to demonstrate that it is our very distance from ideology – whether this is understood in terms of postmodern cynicism or pre-ideological 'enjoyment' – that allows ideology to do its work. The other striking thing about the two books is the way they are able to recast the psychoanalytical concept of fantasy and turn it into a tool for ideological analysis. The French Marxist philosopher Louis Althusser was perhaps the first to show that fantasy is not to be understood as a merely subjective error or delusion, the simple refusal to recognize things as they are. Rather, for Althusser, fantasy is *objective*. It is not so much in what we believe as in our external social practices that fantasy is to be found. Thus, in terms of commodity-fetishism, it does not matter that we know money is not an immediate expression of wealth but only an abstracted version of social relations. All that matters is that in our actual behaviour we continue to act as though it is (*SO*, 31). This is the radical meaning behind Marx's analysis of the commodity form: that 'things (commodities) believe in our place' (*SO*, 34). This is also the conclusion to be drawn from Žižek's introduction of Lacan's notion of the split subject to Althusser's concept of interpellation, for what we see is that ideology works in an *unconscious* way, which is not to be understood as saying that its subjects know nothing of it – they do – but that the *form* of their behaviour escapes them (*SO*, 15). They are 'decentred' not because there is some aspect of their behaviour that they misrecognize or misperceive but because from the beginning they are able to act or believe only through the agency of another (not only the Other as embodied in the fetish but also as embodied in social customs [*SO*, 36]).

These two books, although strikingly original in the context of the English-speaking reception of Continental philosophy, were in fact the outcome of a larger body of work done by Žižek and a group of like-minded Yugoslavian theorists, principally centred around the University of Ljubljana, throughout the 1970s and 1980s. (These theorists, with whom Žižek continues to maintain his ties, often either collaborating with them or writing the forewords to their books, include the philosopher Miran Božovič, author of *An Utterly Dark Spot* and editor of Jeremy Bentham's *The Panopticon Writings*; philosopher Mladen Dolar, author of *The Bone in the Spirit: A Lacanian Reading of Hegel's 'Phenomenology of Spirit'* and co-author with Žižek of *Opera's Second Death*; legal theorist Renata Salecl, author of *The Spoils of Freedom* and *(Per)versions of Love and Hate*; and philosopher Alenka Zupančič, author of *Ethics of the Real: Kant, Lacan.*) Žižek in interviews speaks of the various orientations of philosophy in the former Yugoslavia against which he and his colleagues pitched themselves:

In the Republic of Slovenia, there were two predominant philosophical approaches: Frankfurt School Marxism and Heideggerianism. Both were unacceptable to us Lacanians, not only generally, but in Slovenia the Communist Party was intelligent enough to adopt Frankfurt School Marxism as its official ideology. Heideggerianism was from the beginning linked to right-wing populism, and in other parts of Yugoslavia to the darkest Stalinist forces. For us, Althusser was crucial.[4]

Why Althusser? Because the old Yugoslavia was the proverbial 'socialism with a human face', in which the problem was not the direct imposition of ideology but the fact that the old regime did not appear to take its own ideology seriously, and incorporated its own criticism in advance (*IR*, 3). It is exactly the same problem of private cynicism and public obedience that we find in contemporary capitalism (with same question of why this cynicism, far from undermining the regime's hold on power, actually strengthens it).

Indeed, after studying at the University of Ljubljana, Žižek was at first unable to find a job teaching because he was deemed by the authorities to be 'too unreliable'. He spent a number of years in the 1970s unemployed, before finally, his intellectual brilliance unable to be denied, but prevented from having any actual contact with students, he was given a research position at the Institute of Sociology attached to the University. Žižek now ironically describes this period – during which he was supported by the state but not forced into normal academic duties – 'in Michael J. Fox terms as the secret of my success'.[5] It is a situation he has been able to maintain, thanks to his frenetic publishing schedule and his burgeoning world-wide reputation:

> Every three years I write a research proposal. I then divide it into three one-sentence paragraphs, which I call my yearly projects.
> At the end of each year I change my research project's future tense verbs into the past tense and then call it my yearly report. With total freedom, I am a total workaholic.[6]

After obtaining a Doctorate in Philosophy at the University of Ljubljana in 1981, Žižek then went to Paris to study at the famous Seminar of Lacan's designated heir Jacques-Alain Miller, by whom he was analysed and with whom he would take out a Doctorate in Psychoanalysis in 1985. The book *Le Plus Sublime des Hystériques – Hegel passe* (1988) is a product of Žižek's French period, in which he first puts forward his unique blend of Lacan and popular culture, as well as his unorthodox reading of Hegel. (It also includes much of what was to become *Sublime Object* and *For They Know Not*.) It sees Hegel not, as a generation of French post-structuralists have, as a thinker of the dialectical reconciliation of opposites, but as the most profound theorist of difference – a difference that is not to be grasped directly but only through the very failure of identity (*HP*, 89–90).

Immediately following *For They Know Not*, three new books appear. They are the first we would say that specifically come about as a result of Žižek's new English-speaking audience, that are not simply the outcome of his previous study or personal circumstances. They are perhaps less charged politically, less filled with the urgency of their task. As their titles indicate, they are essentially popularizations – virtuosic, pop-encyclopaedic, sublime-bathetic couplings of the highest and the lowest cultural themes. *Looking Awry: An Introduction to Lacan through Popular Culture* (1991) leads the reader through a number of Lacanian concepts ('Real', 'Gaze', 'Sinthome') by illustrating them with examples taken from popular culture. Thus we have Steven Spielberg's *Empire of the Sun* used to speak of the 'answer of the Real' (*LA*, 29–30), Michael Mann's *Manhunter* to speak of the perverse 'gaze' (*LA*, 107–8) and Patricia Highsmith's short story 'The Pond' to speak of the pathological 'sinthome' (*LA*, 133–6). This is followed by *Enjoy Your Symptom! Jacques Lacan in Hollywood and Out* (1992), which consists of a series of two-part lectures, the first elaborating some Lacanian concept through an example taken from Hollywood cinema – what Žižek calls 'for the other' – and the second treating the same concept in terms of its inherent content – 'in itself' (*E!*, xi). Thus we have a discussion of Lacan's notion of the suicidal 'act' through a consideration of the films of Roberto Rossellini (*E!*, 31–66), the postmodern loss of the 'phallus' in terms of David Lynch's *Elephant Man* (*E!*, 113–46) and woman as a 'symptom' of man with regard to the *femmes fatales* of 1950s film noir (*E!*, 149–93). The third book that appears in English during this period, although it was originally published in French in 1988, is the edited anthology *Everything You Always Wanted to Know about Lacan (But Were Afraid to Ask Hitchcock)* (1992). It includes essays by the French film critic Pascal Bonitzer on Hitchcockian suspense, Zupančič on the way in which 'theatre' reveals the truth in Hitchcock and a long essay by Žižek on how the spectator's gaze is already included in Hitchcock's films. All of these books, which are absolute academic bestsellers and begin to bring his name for the first time before a wider audience, establish Žižek's lasting popular public image as a devoted pop-culture aficionado. There appears to be in his work a deliberate inversion of aesthetic categories, an upending of cultural hierarchies. Thus we have the putting together of Stephen King and Sophocles (*LA*, 25–6), Wagner and Westerns (*LA*, 114–15) and McCullough and Kant (*LA*, 160–62). There is obviously a kind of provocation to all of this, very close to that distinctive postmodern sensibility of camp, but Žižek claims an exalted pedigree for his procedure: Diogenes, Walter Benjamin and even Kant himself (*LA*, vii).

The year 1993 saw the publication of arguably Žižek's *magnum opus*, the extraordinary *Tarrying with the Negative: Kant, Hegel and the Critique of Ideology*. In it, we find his most extended treatment of Hegel so far, again arguing, against a whole generation of post-structuralists in general and Derrida in particular, that Hegel does not attempt to do away with all difference within a 'restricted' economy but rather seeks to theorize a fundamental 'crack' in the world, which forever resists dialectical synthesis (*TN*, 21). In the chapter 'Hegel's "Logic of Essence" as a Theory of Ideology', Žižek makes the case for the importance of Hegel's notion of 'positing the presuppositions' (*TN*, 126) for any serious work in ideology analysis. He also looks at the way Hegel reconceptualizes Kant's notion of the 'sublime' not as some transcendental 'beyond' *out there* but as a kind of fantasy image brought about by a split *in here* (*TN*, 35–9). This strange logic, which Žižek will go on to connect with a certain feminine 'not-all', as opposed to a masculine 'universality produced through exception' (*TN*, 53–8), will have the widest implications for the rest of Žižek's work. It will allow him to criticize, for example, the usual notion of human rights as a universality only possible on the basis of a series of exclusions (women, children, the mad, the primitive), a universality from which ultimately everybody is excluded (*ME*, 157–8), as opposed to a conception of human rights as non-universal but applying precisely to these exceptions (*L*, 267–8). Or it will allow him to think why, although any opposition to it is swallowed up or absorbed by it, the current capitalist order is necessarily incomplete, unable to be realized (*TS*, 358; *L*, 266–7).

This interest in a particular 'feminine' logic is continued in the subsequent *Metastases of Enjoyment: Six Essays on Woman and Causality* (1994), the first of three new books that have a partial, essay-like quality after the systematic exposition of *Tarrying with the Negative*. In *Metastases*, Žižek explores this logic in a number of fields, from the masculine construction of woman in mediaeval courtly poetry and film noir to the radical 'feminism' (in a typically perverse and counter-intuitive reading) of Otto Weininger's notorious turn-of-the-nineteenth-century anti-Semitic and misogynistic tract *Sex and Character*. In *Metastases*, following it must be said the pioneering Lacanian feminist Joan Copjec, Žižek takes a distance from the usual 'constructivist' accounts of contemporary feminism, which argue that woman is merely a performatively enacted or historically contingent fiction. For Žižek, this essentially 'symbolic' conception of woman – which condemns her either to mimic parodically the various clichés of femininity or to a silence outside of language – excludes the 'Real' of sexual difference. Rather, instead of this choice, what we see, to put it in Žižek's still too-condensed formulation, is that, whereas 'it is man who is wholly submitted to the phallus (since positing an exception is the way to maintain its universal domination), only woman through the inconsistency of her desire attains the domain "beyond the phallus"' (*ME*, 160–61).

Žižek's next book, *The Indivisible Remainder: An Essay on Schelling and Related Matters* (1996), both signals a shift in his work and makes explicit what was previously only implicit in it. It is an extended analysis of a now slightly marginal figure from the history of German philosophy, F.W.J. Schelling (1775–1854). Žižek's polemical point is that Schelling in fact played a pivotal role between the idealism of Kant and Hegel and the materialism of Marx (*IR*, 4). But in what exactly does this materialism consist? Žižek insists that tracking it down is a tricky business. It is not to be seen where we might expect. It is to be found in that moment in Schelling when he admits that God is not eternally given but has as it were to posit Himself, contract Himself out of some obscure impenetrable 'Ground' (*IR*, 61–2). That is, Schelling is concerned not with the problem of how to pass from the perfect to the imperfect, how God enters the world, but on the contrary with the problem of how to pass from the imperfect to the perfect, how God arises in the first place (*IR*, 16, 112–13). Schelling's crucial realization is that God is *imperfect*, that there is always something missing from Him: a gap that might be understood as the human itself (*IR*, 67). It is a realization that Schelling himself came to shrink from. By means of an analysis of the successive drafts of the great *Weltalter* fragment (whose unfinished character for Žižek is the very sign of its materialist status), Žižek shows how Schelling moves from a position in which God comes about through a primordial contraction of 'Ground', which is materialist, to one in which God is a kind of pre-existing essence, which is idealist. And in 1997 Žižek reissues as *The Abyss of Freedom*, accompanied by a long introduction written by him, Schelling's second draft of the *Weltalter* fragment, in which his thinking of this 'free' positing by God of His own existence goes furthest, and draws a perhaps surprising conclusion: that materialism is not to be understood as a form of determinism, in which everything can be exhaustively explained, but as what keeps causality open, what allows the possibility of freedom.

Also in 1997 *The Plague of Fantasies* is published, which is very much a collection of disparate pieces, including a version of the introduction first written for the collection *Mapping Ideology* (1994) and essays on such diverse topics as virtual reality, the sexual act in cinema and the possibility of an ethics beyond the Good. (*Indivisible Remainder*, for its part, already included an essay entitled 'Quantum Physics with Lacan'!) It is interesting to observe here how Žižek has moved on from his earlier attempts to analyse ideology in terms of the fetish in *Sublime Object* and *For They Know Not*. Even bearing in mind the vastly expanded, intra-psychic conception of ideology at stake there, in *Plague* it is even more intrusive and extreme. We have the sense of something that penetrates even the deepest recesses of our bodies, that colonizes even our most private fantasies. We have an 'interpassivity', as in computer games and simulations, in which the Other not only knows and believes for us but even enjoys for us (*PF*, 113–17). It is a world in which we risk psychosis because that gap between the world and our various constructions of it becomes increasingly filled in (*PF*, 157–9). Ideology becomes a total and seamless screen, as we realize that what we understand by 'reality' was always already virtual. And yet, says Žižek – in a formulation that might remind us of Jean Baudrillard – this is only because of a certain 'Real' that is excluded (*PF*, 163). It is at this point that another 'ethics', an 'ethics' beyond the Good, might be thought.

The *Ticklish Subject: The Absent Centre of Political Ontology*, published in 1999, is another attempted *summa* of Žižek's philosophy. This massive, 400-page tome, reputedly written in a mere six months, is divided up into three parts: the first, which treats Heidegger and his reading of the Kantian Transcendental Imagination in *Kant and the Problem of Metaphysics* (this a continuation of the enquiry into that 'gap' which allows freedom in Schelling); the second, which takes up the fate of three post-Althusserian French political thinkers (Alain Badiou, Etienne Balibar and Jacques Rancière); and the third, which consists of an extended engagement with the feminist deconstructionist Judith Butler. Or, as Žižek says in his Introduction, the book addresses three distinctive philosophical traditions: German philosophical Idealism; French political philosophy; and Anglo-American cultural studies (*TS*, 5). *Ticklish Subject* marks an advance on Žižek's previous work in several respects. First, the opening section sees a detailed explication of the thought of Heidegger, who is to become a more and more common reference in Žižek's writings to come. Second, following the path-breaking book by Badiou, *St Paul, or, The Birth of Universalism*, Žižek is more and more willing to define his political project – against Laclau and Mouffe – in terms of a certain universality. Third, the book constitutes Žižek's closest encounter yet with feminist-queer 'constructivism' and a defence against the emerging criticism that his use of the Lacanian 'Real' is 'ahistorical'. We see him in his debate with Butler seeking to negotiate a way simultaneously against historicism and any simple anti-historicism.

And all of this he does, finally, by means of a spirited and unexpected defence of Cartesian subjectivity, the object of critique of virtually every contemporary philosophical orientation (deconstructionism, feminism, New Age spiritualism, scientific cognitivism).

This is followed soon after — with no sign of fatigue or let-down — by the short polemical pamphlet *The Fragile Absolute, or, Why is the Christian Legacy Worth Fighting For?* (2000). It can be seen as a continuation of *Ticklish Subject*'s defence of Pauline Christianity and its insight (as opposed to multiculturalism, ethical relativism and even orthodox Christianity) that a universal truth is worth fighting for. It is a truth, however, that is only to be obtained from a position of engaged particularity. In this we might see a shift from the earlier defence of the 'absolute particular' (*LA*, 156) of the other's enjoyment, akin perhaps to traditional liberal tolerance, to an assertion of the 'particular absolute' of our own partisan position, akin to St Paul's famous militancy. This argument for a newly committed 'universality' is seen also in *Did Somebody Say Totalitarianism?*, which appears the following year. This book is a withering attack upon the contemporary tendency to level the charge of 'totalitarianism' against any attempt to propose a political 'Grand Narrative', an accusation that functions precisely as a way of discouraging any real social change (for example, the argument that any attempt to propose a unified political position against capitalism can only lead to a new form of dictatorship). At this point a more and more explicit Marxism enters Žižek's work, indeed, an argument for a form of communism involving an organized party structure and the socialization of economic resources. Žižek's politics here have moved well beyond any notion of an always unrealizable 'democracy', in which the locus of power must always remain empty (*TK*, 267–70), to an admiration for such figures as Lenin, who were willing to seize power and impose their political will. But it is a Lenin, surprisingly — as Žižek argues in the long Afterword he writes for his 2002 collection of Lenin texts, *Revolution at the Gates* — who is not at all inconsistent with a certain notion of Christianity.

Throughout this period, Žižek continues to publish a whole series of other texts and interventions: an essay on David Lynch, a long-time favourite, *The Art of the Ridiculous Sublime* (2000); a lecture series on the Polish director Krzysztof Kieślowski for the British Film Institute, *The Fright of Real Tears* (2001); a short text updating his thoughts on ideology, *On Belief* (2001); a response to the attacks on the World Trade Center, *Welcome to the Desert of the Real!* (2002); essays in books he has either edited himself or been included in, *On the Gaze and Voice as Love*

Objects (1996), *Cogito and the Unconscious* (1998) and *Sexuation* (2002); a joint volume with Butler and Laclau, in which each debates the others' position, *Contingency, Hegemony, Universality* (2000). It is simply an extraordinary outpouring of material, which shows no signs of slowing down and, indeed, even seems to be speeding up. In 2000, Žižek publishes three books; in 2001, four; in 2002, four again. One of the paradoxes of this is that it seems that, as his work becomes more and more explicitly anti-capitalist, it is also becoming more commodified. That is, we might not only speak of Žižek himself in terms of a certain excremental identification, but also of his work. In its very excessiveness, unmasterability, relentless accumulation and the difficulty of knowing what to do with it all, does it not resemble excrement, or even the hoarding of capital itself? It is a paradox he explores in his recent work: that not only is capitalism its own critique but this critique always ends up returning to capital itself (*L*, 277). But Žižek could only get the effects he does by going as close as possible to his own personal dissolution, his fusion with the Other. As he writes in *Ticklish Subject*:

> This is the domain 'beyond the Good', in which a human being encounters the death-drive as the utmost limit of human experience, and pays the price by undergoing a radical 'subjective destitution', by being reduced to an excremental remainder. Lacan's point is that this limit-experience is the irreducible/constitutive condition of the (im)possibility of the creative act of embracing a Truth-Event; it opens up and sustains the space for the Truth-Event, yet its excess always threatens to undermine it. (*TS*, 161)

How to read Žižek?

Of course, it is absurd to suggest that a thinker as prolific and popular as Žižek needs an introduction. After all, what can any commentary say about him that he does not already say? How to explain Žižek any more clearly than he does himself? (Or, to put this another way, what is to guarantee that we can make any clearer what Žižek fails to? How can we be sure that we get to the bottom of what drives him on through all those endless repetitions and re-elaborations that run throughout his texts?) In that process of radical externalization that characterizes Žižek's work, this striving to make himself absolutely clear, Žižek compares what he is doing to the Lacanian procedure of the *passe*, in which the analyst-in-training has to pass on their findings to two uninitiated members of the general public, who in turn have to transmit them to the examining committee. 'The idiot', he says generously, 'for whom I attempt to formulate a theoretical point as clearly as possible is ultimately myself' (*ME*, 175). But it is undoubtedly also us. Perhaps all we can offer in this book, paradoxically, is to make Žižek *less* accessible, *less* popular, *less* easily understood. We do not try to find other examples to explain his work – always a worthless academic exercise. We do not try to write in the same exuberant style. We do not try to be funny. (Think of all those endless, dreadful attempts to imitate Derridean *écriture*.) In a sense, we try to be faithful to Žižek's own self-assessment from his Preface to the collection *The Žižek Reader*:

> In contrast to the cliché of the academic writer beneath whose impassive style the reader can catch an occasional glimpse of a so-called lively personality, I always perceived myself as the author of books whose excessively 'witty' texture serves as the envelope of a fundamental coldness, of a 'machinic' deployment of a line of thought which follows its path with utter indifference towards the pathology of so-called human considerations. (*ZR*, viii)

But what is this 'machine'? What is the internal, non-human, non-pathological logic of Žižek's work? Here we meet perhaps the second difficulty that arises in any consideration of Žižek. Introductory texts like this one inevitably excuse themselves before the author they discuss. In a mock-heroic version of Hegel's *Phenomenology of Spirit*, they wish only to disappear before the greatness they present. In a performative contradiction, they are nothing, they insist. It is much better to read the 'real' author; their only hope is that the person buying their book goes on to read the 'real' author; and so on. But is this really the case with Žižek? In another side to that radical externalization we spoke of before, is it not possible that Žižek's own books are merely, as he himself puts it, an 'introduction to Lacan through popular culture' or 'everything you always wanted to know about Lacan (but were afraid to ask Hitchcock)'? That is to say, is there any point in actually reading Žižek? Might there ultimately be no difference in status between our introduction to Žižek and Žižek himself? And might this not even be to suggest that there is no need to read Žižek if we have already read those authors he writes about? Perhaps this book should be entitled *Everything You Always Wanted to Know about Žižek (But Were Too Lazy to Read Žižek)* or *Everything You Already Knew about Žižek (Because You Have Already Read Lacan and Hegel)*.

At stake here is the status of Žižek's thought. Is there anything beneath the glittering brilliance of its writerly surface, its extraordinary and eclectic range of references, its argumentative brio? Is it merely an extended explication of Lacan, a fusion of Lacan and Hegel, a politicization of Lacan through Marx? Does it possess that 'oneness' or unifying trait that we take to characterize all authentic philosophy? Or must all this be thought another way? *Is* significant thought characterized by any identifiable oneness, or is it rather always split, introducing a kind of split into the world? And is this what Žižek's thought forces us to consider? Is it something like this 'doubling' or 'antagonism' that is at stake in it? In order to answer these questions, let us listen in fact to the words of one of Žižek's critics, the 'post-theory' film writer Ed O'Neill. Here he is reviewing the Žižek-edited anthology *Cogito and the Unconscious*:

> Example after example is supplied, but the principle that makes them examples is not itself given. Appeals are implicitly made to Lacan's authority, but the source of that authority is never mentioned. The truth of Lacan's theories is urged by showing how other people's theories support that truth but without explaining why these theories have the same object. One concept is defined in terms of another, which is then described the same way, *ad infinitum*. What's being explained is mixed with what's doing the explaining in a circular fashion so striking that it may well count as both a novelty and a technical innovation in the history of interpretation.[7]

What exactly is going on here? O'Neill in his *naïveté* perhaps comes close to putting his finger on the two striking though contradictory impressions we have when reading Žižek. The first is that, as in the confusion of theory and examples he observes, it is not some literal fidelity to Lacan's psychoanalysis that is at stake there. It is not some pre-existing orthodoxy or body of precepts that is being 'applied' to various examples. Rather, Lacanian psychoanalysis is caught up from the beginning in other fields of knowledge, establishing a potentially endless series of analogies between them: 'One concept is defined in terms of another, which is then described the same way, *ad infinitum*.' And this undoubtedly has the strange effect that, even when Žižek is not directly speaking about Lacan, he is speaking about Lacan. Lacan is not so much being translated as he is the very medium of translation itself. The second impression we have is that the total presence of Lacan in Žižek's work means that his actual authority disappears. Just as with that confusion between theory and examples O'Neill observes, there is a confusion between Lacan and those who cite him: 'The truth of Lacan's theories is urged by showing how other people's theories support that truth.' That is to say, it is precisely through Žižek's dogmatic fidelity to Lacan, through his absolute identification with him, that he is able to become original himself. Unlike so many other commentators who through their criticisms of Lacan reveal themselves to be attached to him, it is only Žižek who through his literal adherence to him is finally able to break with him.[8] As Žižek says, it is our very desire to look for mistakes and inconsistencies in the Other that testifies to the fact that we still transfer on to them, while it is only something like this identification with the symptom that might allow us to traverse the fantasy (SO, 66). Or, to put this in the slightly blasphemous form of the Jesuits' relationship to God, Žižek 'believes that the success of his undertaking depends entirely on him and in no way on [Lacan]; but, nonetheless, sets to work as if [Lacan] alone will do everything and he himself nothing' (B, 125).

What is radically posed by Žižek's work – both as a theme within it and by the very existence of the work itself – is the relationship of thought to the Other, to the subject who knows. How to become original when one's great influence is Lacan, who has already thought of everything (not so much because he actually has as because, within the structure of transference that characterizes thought, he will be seen as having already done so)? Let us take here the example of those two thinkers who are constantly invoked in this regard, Marx and Freud. It is they who are seen to constitute an unsurpassable horizon to thought, impossible to go beyond. It is they whom we can only ever be seen to repeat. But what is it that characterizes the particular quality of their thought? And how is it that we might somehow think 'after' it? The specific concepts that Marx and Freud introduce, class and the unconscious, are not simply empirical, demonstrably either true or not, but rather challenge the very limits of scientificity. In a way, they 'double' what is by an undemonstrable yet irrefutable hypothesis that not only lies within the existing discursive field but also resituates it, giving all the elements within it a different meaning. As a result, these concepts are present when they appear to be absent (the field as it is is only possible because of them) and absent when they most appear present (any naming of them from within the current set-up is only to stand in for them). So what could it mean, therefore, to relate to Marx and Freud, to continue their work, as perhaps Althusser and Lacan did? It must mean that what they do has a similar quality, that it does not so much either follow or refute them as 'double' them, at once completing them and showing that they must be understood for an entirely different reason than the one they give themselves. And it is this that we would say characterizes all significant 'postmodern' thought: the problem of what to say about closed systems, systems of which there is no external standard of judgement, in which the Other already knows everything. (The whole question of the 'end to metaphysics' is misunderstood – even by Badiou and Deleuze – if it is not grasped in this sense.) It is this that distinguishes all philosophical thought worthy of the name: the fact that it does not merely lie within the empirical field but is also the 'transcendental' condition of it. And it is this that constitutes the unity and originality of this thought – not that it is 'one' but that it endlessly doubles and splits the world (and itself): Derrida's *différance*, Deleuze's deterritorialization, Irigaray's woman, Baudrillard's seduction and perhaps something in Žižek . . .

In fact, Hegel was the first philosopher to speak of this 'end' of philosophy. This 'doubling', as Žižek so brilliantly brings out, is what is at stake in Hegel's notion of dialectics and not any reconciliation with the world. And, indeed, it is something like this 'end of philosophy' in the sense of having nothing to say that we see in undoubtedly one of the most interesting attempts to account for what is 'original' about Žižek: Denise Gigante's 'Toward a Notion of Critical Self-Creation: Slavoj Žižek and the "Vortex of Madness" '. She writes: 'But where Žižek is unique, and where he makes his radical break with other literary theorists who take up a position, any position at all that pretends to some notional content or critical truth, is in the fact that he fundamentally has no position.'[9] This, we would say, is a fascinating insight; but we disagree with Gigante when she suggests that this condition is somehow unique to Žižek himself. On the contrary, we would argue that all post-Hegelian philosophy, or indeed all philosophy in the light of Hegel, begins with this 'nothing to say'. It is what we will come to speak of as the 'contraction' of the primordial void in Schelling (*IR*, 22–7). It is that 'empty' speech that for Lacan precedes and makes possible 'full' or authentic speech (*S1*, 51). It is even that *vouloir-dire* or undeconstructible 'Yes!' that motivates deconstruction in Derrida. It is at once an attempt to follow or be faithful to what is, adding nothing, and it is the saying or re-marking of this nothing as something, thus opening up the possibility of something to say. (It is perhaps no coincidence that Lacan speaks of the special status of the great philosophers' knowledge, the way it advances not singly but always 'two by two, in a supposed Other' (*S20*, 97), mentioning in this regard Marx, Freud and even himself, in the Seminar *Encore*, devoted to the question of woman. For, as we will see, this structure in which the symbolic order is total, allowing no exception, and yet we are entirely outside of it, unindebted to any Other, is precisely the 'feminine' logic Lacan is trying to elaborate there.)

Žižek gives another hint as to what he considers philosophical originality – the difference between authentic philosophy and mere academic commentary – in his book on Kieślowski, *The Fright of Real Tears*. He writes: 'In philosophy, it is one thing to talk about, report on, say, the history of the notion of the subject (accompanied by all the proper bibliographical footnotes), even to supplement it with comparative critical remarks; it is quite another to work in theory, to elaborate the notion of the "subject" itself' (*K*, 9). Žižek speaks here of the elaboration of the philosophical notion of the subject as an *example* of the distinction he is proposing between first- and second-order philosophical systems; but we suggest that it is more than an example: it is the very distinction itself. To elaborate the subject *is* what philosophy does. But what exactly does this mean, to elaborate the subject? And in what ways, if any, does Žižek do it? It would involve not only elaborating a particular subject as the name of a philosophical system or a philosophy that will come to be known by a particular name, but – although this is not strictly speaking opposed – the subject as a *split subject*, what Lacan indicates by the symbol $, the subject as gap or void. All significant philosophical systems, that is, introduce a certain gap or void into what is – a gap or void that we would call the subject. Repeating the essential Hegelian gesture of translating 'substance as subject', what is is understood as standing in for a void (*SO*, 201–30; *TN*, 21–7). And it is around this 'subject' that the essential connection between philosophy and psychoanalysis might be made. It is around this 'subject' – the subject as split and the subject as introducing a kind of split – that the originality of Žižek's philosophy is to be found.

'Why is Every Act a Repetition?'

But in order to see what all of this might mean in more detail, let us turn to a text of Žižek's originally entitled 'Philosophy Traversed by Psychoanalysis', and now reprinted in *Enjoy Your Symptom!* as 'Why is Every Act a Repetition?' In this text, Žižek addresses the relationship of psychoanalysis to philosophy, which is precisely not a matter of psychoanalysing philosophy or particular philosophers but of psychoanalysis constituting philosophy's *frame*. As he writes: 'It [psychoanalysis] circumscribes the discourse's frame, i.e., the intersubjective constellation, the relationship toward the teacher, toward authority, which renders possible the philosophical discourse' (*E!*, 92). That is, if psychoanalysis is external to philosophy, it is an externality philosophy cannot do without and which philosophy from the beginning takes as its subject – Žižek in his text cites Plato's *Symposium* as the first attempt by philosophy to speak of its intersubjective (psychoanalytic) origins. In 'Why is Every Act?', however, it is a short text by Kierkegaard, *Philosophical Fragments*, that Žižek considers at greatest length in order to speak of this transferential aspect to philosophy. In *Philosophical Fragments*, Kierkegaard makes a distinction between *theology* (not psychoanalysis) and philosophy (even Plato) over the question of this transferential, intersubjective relationship to truth. Whereas in traditional philosophy, according to Kierkegaard, a philosopher like Socrates is only the 'midwife' for a timeless and eternal truth, in Christian *doxa* the truth of a statement lies not in what is said but in the authority of the one who speaks. The truth of Christ's message lies not in any actual content but in the very fact that Christ said it. This is the meaning behind Kierkegaard's insistence, undoubtedly a little strange to our ears, that anyone who believes what Christ is saying because of what He says reveals themselves not to be a Christian: a Christian, on the contrary, believes what Christ says because it is said by Christ (*E!*, 93).

However, it is not quite as simple as this, for at the same time as this absolute emphasis on Christ's personal authority, He is also only an empty vessel for the word of another. In other words, Christ only possesses the authority He does because He carries the higher, transcendent Word of God. It would be in what He transmits and not in Christ Himself that His power lies. Or, to use Kierkegaard's distinction, Christ is not so much a 'genius' as an 'apostle' (*E!*, 93). (We might think again here of what Lacan says in *Encore* about those special agents of knowledge, Marx, Freud and implicitly himself: that, if they are great and singular figures, whose ideas cannot be separated from them as founders, it is also 'clearly on the basis of the Other that they have constituted the letter at their own expense' (*S*20, 97–8).) We thus appear to have a kind of dilemma, for the authority of Christ lies not in what He says but only in His personal authority, and yet He only retains this authority in so far as He transmits directly and without mediation the Word of God. What then lies at the impossible intersection of these two sets – Christ's life and His teachings? How to think together these two elements that at once exclude and are necessary to each other? Žižek seeks to represent what is at stake by means of the following diagram (*E!*, 96):

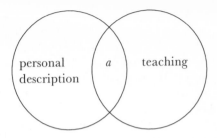

What is important about this diagram? In the first part of his essay, Žižek takes up the question of what Lacan calls the 'forced choice' (*E!*, 69): the idea that underlying the symbolic order in which we live there is a choice whether to enter it or not. As a result of this choice – which in a sense is forced because the only alternative to it is psychosis – a situation that arises after it is able to be presented as though it already existed before it. A situation that relies upon the assent of the subject is able to be presented as though the subject is unnecessary, as though the decision has already been made for them. For example, we recognize the king because he is the king, even though he is the king only because we recognize him. Or we acknowledge the interpellation or hailing of authority – 'Hey you!', as shouted by a policeman – even though it is specifically meant for us only after we acknowledge it.[10] And this 'conversion' of the arbitrary and conventional into the regular and natural is made possible by what Žižek calls the *master-signifier*: that by which an implicit order or prescription is made to seem as though it is only the description of a previously existing state of affairs. As he writes in 'Why is Every Act?': 'The Lacanian S1, the "master-signifier" which represents the subject for other signifiers, is therefore the point of intersection between the performative and the constative, i.e., the point at which the "pure" performative coincides with (assumes the form of) its opposite' (*E!*, 99). Žižek's point, however, is that in a way we can *repeat* this forced choice and thus expose this process. We can go back to that moment of our original entry into the symbolic and relive it as though it has not already taken place, and thus think what is lost by it.[11]

It is this possibility, Žižek argues, that is to be seen in Kierkegaard's conception of our relationship to Christ. What we glimpse there in the laying bare of the transferential relationship to knowledge, in the way the Word of Christ relies upon a certain blind authority, is a moment 'before' we enter the symbolic order, as though we could somehow choose whether to recognize the king or accept that interpellation by

which we become a subject. (Of course, the paradox of this is that there is
in fact no 'choice' involved here at all, because we only become subjects
possessed of free will *as a result of* this decision to enter the symbolic order.
And it is precisely in this split not so much between various choices *within*
the symbolic as *between* the symbolic and what comes 'before' it that
the subject in the proper philosophical sense emerges. As Žižek writes:
'In this split, in this impossibility of a "pure" performative, the subject of
the signifier emerges'. [*E!*, 99]) In other words, according to Žižek, what
we witness in Kierkegaard's model of Christian authority, with its absolute emphasis on the physical presence of Christ, is a momentary
'separation' of prescription and description, something that is not
simply reducible to the symbolic order. And this is why, in that diagram
above, Žižek represents the intersection between 'personal description'
(prescription) and 'teaching' (description), which would normally be
occupied by S1 or the master-signifier, by what Lacan calls *object a* or a
'little piece of the real' (*E!*, 101). Again, as opposed to traditional philosophy, in which the teacher or the means of expression is finally dispen-
sable as the mere medium of an eternal truth, in Kierkegaard it is the
unsurpassable condition for access to Christian revelation, which is not
to be grasped outside of the actual present in which it occurs.

For Žižek, it is just this emphasis on the material presence of the analyst that also characterizes psychoanalysis, and why that 'trauma' it
diagnoses is not merely to be understood as some repressed and timeless
memory the analyst helps us to recover but as something that is played
out for real within the psychoanalytic session, something that does not
exist before analysis and actual contact with the analyst (*E!*, 102).
And, again, it is this 'repetition' of the forced choice that might allow
psychoanalysis, like Christianity, to *break* the transferential relationship,
to bring out the separation between the analyst and the position they
occupy, to see the prescription (transference, personal authority)
'before' it becomes description (the way things naturally appear to be,
teaching). It is not perhaps here simply a matter of getting rid of the
master-signifier, for the symbolic field is unable to be constituted without it – again, the question of the paradoxical split 'subject' – but of
somehow rendering present that empty prescription that 'precedes' and
'allows' it. As Žižek observes of Lacan's clinical practice and the way he
attempted to theorize the position of the analyst as holding the position
of *object a* in that diagram above:

> The unmasking of the master's imposture does not abolish the place
> he occupies, it just renders it visible in its original emptiness, i.e., as

preceding the element which fills it out. Therefore the Lacanian notion of the analyst *qua envers* (reverse) of the master: of somebody who holds the place of the master, yet who, by means of his (non)activity, undermines the master's charisma, suspends the effect of 'quilting', and thus renders visible the distance that separates the master from the place he occupies, i.e., the radical contingency of the subject who occupies this place. (*E!*, 103)

And the same would go for all great thinkers in the relationship of their personal authority to their teaching: they too ultimately seek to 'render visible the distance that separates the master from the place he occupies'.[12] It is this that constitutes the anti-authoritarian thrust of our contemporary 'masters of suspicion'.

Yet, as Žižek is undoubtedly aware, Marx, Freud and Lacan are not straightforwardly anti-authoritarian or anti-transferential. In fact, what their work – which is arguably the final outcome of that critique of authority that characterizes the Enlightenment – reveals is that the Enlightenment is not, as is usually thought, opposed to authority but inseparable from it. The truth is arrived at not through the careful weighing up of the reasons for and against a certain proposition, but by the unappealable fiat of authority. Indeed, as we have already seen, in so far as the statements of these thinkers are not just empirical but also assert the 'transcendental' conditions of their respective fields, they cannot be tested or questioned but only followed. As Žižek writes:

Since Marx and Freud opened up a new theoretical field which sets the very criteria of veracity, their work cannot be put to the test in the same way one is allowed to question the statements of their followers ... For that reason, every 'further development' of Marxism or psychoanalysis necessarily assumes the form of a 'return' to Marx and Freud: the form of a (re)discovery of some hitherto overlooked layer of their work, i.e., of bringing to light what the founders 'produced without knowing what they produced'. (*E!*, 100)

But it is at this point that we must ask: why this coincidence of transference and anti-transference? Why are these master-thinkers not simply anti-transferential but also transferential, indeed more transferential than ordinary thinkers? Is it not merely that the authority of transference is to be overcome by another transference but that the very attempt to uncover transference leads to transference? And how, to come back to our original question of Žižek's relationship to his sources, are we to imagine Žižek 'going beyond' them, when every 'further development' of them can only assume the form of a 'return' to them, a '(re)discovery of some hitherto overlooked layer' of their work? Can any such 'breaking with' or 'overturning of' them only take the form of a certain 'return' to them? And what, finally, is the role of *object a* in all of this? Is it to be thought of as exposing the 'original emptiness preceding the element that fills it out' in that diagram above, or must all this be thought another way?

In order to begin answering these questions, let us turn to the passage in 'Why is Every Act?' immediately after Žižek discusses the attempted psychoanalytic breaking of the transference. He speaks there of the Lacanian procedure of the *passe*, in which, as we have seen, the analyst-in-training does not immediately pass on their findings to the examining committee but only through two uninvolved middle-persons or *passeurs*. In this way, Lacan sought to break any initiatic contact between the analyst and the committee; but there is also something else produced. For, of course, these *passeurs* get things wrong, distort the message. The message does not arrive intact at its destination. And yet, if we can say this, this just *is* the knowledge of the unconscious that the analyst-in-training possesses. It is just *this* that they are able to pass on intact to the examining committee. In other words, the knowledge of the unconscious that the analyst possesses lies not so much in anything they actually say as in their saying of it. It is nothing that can be lost or distorted because it *is* this very loss and distortion. And it is this, finally, that the analyst-in-training must realize – just as earlier we spoke about the way that 'trauma' does not exist as something recollected but as what is produced in the relationship with the analyst – that the meaning of their words is nothing that can be grasped by them but comes about only in the relationship between two. This is the experience of 'decentrement' that Lacan called 'subjective destitution', which is the realization that our meaning does not originate with ourselves but only with our mistakes and distortions, as what we have produced without knowing it or what is in us more than ourselves. That is to say, what the analyst must in the end realize is that they are themselves a *passeur*: that they transmit knowledge from the Other to the Other without knowing what it is; that all they add is a certain distortion, a particular way of speaking, a characteristic enunciation.

Do we not see the same thing with our great philosophers? For perhaps unexpectedly – to go back to that original distinction Kierkegaard makes *vis-à-vis* Christ – Žižek calls them at a certain point not 'geniuses' but 'apostles' (*E!*, 101). But of whom are they the apostles? In what way is it not merely a matter of their personal qualities but also of them being the carriers of the word of another? And how is this a clue to what we have just seen about them: that they are unable to be surpassed, or surpassed only in their own name? Again, what is it that defines the particular contribution of our major thinkers? What is it that separates their thought – authentic philosophy – from that of others – academic commentary? If we can repeat ourselves, it is because they do not simply offer concepts from within an already existing field but also redefine this field, or as Žižek puts it they 'circumscribe the discourse's frame'. It is this Žižek calls, with regard to Plato and Kierkegaard – as an example of this – the 'subjective constellation, the relationship toward the teacher, toward authority, which renders possible the philosophical discourse'. But, once more, we would say that this is not so much an *example* of as the very thing that authentic philosophy does: it speaks of, takes into account, the intersubjective dimension of philosophy. It grasps, understands, that from the beginning it is caught up in a transferential – dialogical – relationship with its interpreters. Its word lives on – and it recognizes this – not because of some concrete doctrine set out in advance but because it is seen in retrospect to be what its interpreters say it is. To put this another way, what exactly does Marx mean by class, the specific concept that he introduces? Class is not something that is either present or not, but what is present in its absence and absent in its presence. The meaning and even the existence of class is always being disputed, but class just *is* this struggle (*ME*, 181–3; *T?*, 228). And, similarly, Freud's unconscious, as Lacan demonstrates, is not so much something that is either present or not as what comes about in the relationship between it and its interpreters, whatever it is that they speak of. It is as though Marx and Freud (and Hegel too, as Žižek shows in his *Le Plus Sublime des Hystériques*) have undergone the *passe* and now realize that they are merely the empty transmitters or apostles of the word of another. But of whose word are they the apostles (and this undoubtedly applies to Christ too, as St Paul shows)? Precisely of *us*, their interpreters or analysts.

But, to get back to our main point: the paradox here is that it is in remarking upon transference that our speakers produce transference. It is in speaking of the way that their message is always distorted that their message is never distorted. The intersubjective element of philosophy, the fact that its authority comes from us, is not simply irreconcilable with the authority of philosophy but is its real basis. And this is the ambiguity of *object a* as at once what is in the subject 'more than themselves' and the stand-in for that 'act' that would repeat and thus reveal the 'forced choice'. For let us go back to that 'act' by means of which we are able to relive this forced choice as though it has not yet happened, and which opens us up to something 'before' or 'outside' of the symbolic order. The example Žižek gives of it in 'Why is Every Act?' is Antigone's famous 'No!' to King Creon's refusal to allow her brother Polynices a proper burial. It is a gesture that places her outside of the social, that proposes a radically different set of values, and which therefore can only be judged in its own terms. As Žižek writes: 'This "law" in the name of which Antigone insists on Polynices' right to burial is the law of the "pure" signifier prior to every positive law that judges our deeds: it is the law of the Name which fixes our identity beyond the eternal flow of generation and corruption' (*E!*, 92). And yet, ironically, to all intents and purposes, this 'No!' is exactly like the word of the master-signifier itself, which can also only be judged tautologically and requilts the social field, forcing us to read everything in a new way. And this, again, is the difficulty we have with our master-thinkers and why it is so hard to think 'after' them, for in a sense the concepts they propose are nothing positive but only the 'inscription of a pure difference' (*E!*, 91), already naming their own difference from themselves. That is, as we have seen with the concepts of class and the unconscious, we could no sooner name their absence, our difference from them or even the fact that they arise only in their relationship to us, than these would return to them as what they are already *about*. It is they that would remark before us their own absence and difference from themselves.[13]

As Žižek admits, this standing outside of the forced choice can only end up repeating it. This act comes down finally to a choice not whether to enter the Symbolic or not but between two alternatives already *within* the Symbolic. As Žižek makes clear in that other diagram he reproduces in the chapter (*E!*, 76), *object a* still lies within the set defined by S1 and S2, two different master-signifiers. Or, as he puts it there: 'The subject cannot "have it all" and choose himself as nonbarred; all he can choose is a partial mark, one of two signifiers, the symbolic mandate that will represent him, designate his place in the intersubjective network' (*E!*, 76). Or, as he will elsewhere say, paraphrasing Lacan, the choice comes down to that between 'bad' and 'worse' (*E!*, 75), which perhaps is not simply that between a master-signifier within the symbolic order and a psychotic act outside of it, but is always echoed – in so far as we are a 'split' subject – in the choice between two signifiers within the symbolic order. But it is in this context that we must read Žižek carefully – and perhaps even against himself – when he states that in Lacan's 'suspension' of the master-signifier we might somehow see '[the master's place] visible in its original emptiness, i.e., as preceding the original element which fills it out'. For, as Žižek himself argues, this *object a* only 'comes into being through being lost, i.e., it is not given prior to its loss' (*E!*, 75). In other words, this empty place is never given as such but is only ever a retrospective effect of it being filled in. The repetition of the forced choice never really comes up with a different decision, never actually chooses otherwise; but this repetition itself testifies to something always not chosen. Again, as Žižek says with regard to the notion of the working through of 'trauma' in psychoanalysis, it is not so much some prior existing alternative that is either recollected or not as a fleeting possibility that arises in the present, at the very moment it is not chosen. As in Kierkegaard's notion of the religious, we do not so much repeat some particular thing or even decision as the very failure to make a decision: 'In so far as repetition is not possible, it is possible to repeat the very experience of impossibility' (*E!*, 79). And in repeating it as impossible, we do not merely render it possible, change the course of events, but think what is excluded to ensure that things are as they are, what is allowed by this always unchosen alternative. This is the very 'transcendental' philosophical gesture as such, understanding how what is stands in for a certain fundamental impossibility.

It is for this reason too that this act of which we are speaking is not some 'exception reconciled in the universal' (*E!*, 84), or at least not in any obvious sense. For this repetition of the forced choice is not in the end a breaking or transgression of the symbolic order. It is not directly opposed to or outside of it. As we have already seen, we can only overturn one prescription by another prescription, one transference by another transference. Rather, what this 'possibility' opened up by the act suggests is that, even though there is no actual outside to the symbolic order, even though any attempt to think something prior to it can only choose an alternative already within it, all this is only possible because of a certain 'outside', a certain 'alternative' forever excluded. It is precisely what Žižek means by the Real as a kind of 'transhistorical kernel' (*E!*, 81), for which *object a* stands in. Again, it would not be so much anything prior to the Symbolic as what is excluded at the very moment it is included, what each of these master-signifiers tries to speak of, what each of these 'doublings' or 'requiltings' seeks to respond to. And what this forces us to think is both that there is nothing outside of the symbolic order (this *object a* will always turn into another master-signifier) and that this Symbolic is empty, contains nothing (in a way does not exist until the 'free' decision to enter it). At the very moment the symbolic order 'doubles', names its own difference from itself, there is also something that 'doubles' it, which cannot be named. As opposed to any 'exception reconciled in the universal', there is at once no exception and all is exception. And this is the ambiguity of *object a* as that 'law of the name', let us say of the master-signifier: it is both only a new master-signifier, which cannot be lost, and what allows this loss to be recorded, that without which this loss would not exist. It is this equivalence that Žižek speaks of throughout his work in terms of the Hegelian formulae 'the Spirit is a Bone' (*E!*, 88) and the monarch as the identity of the 'state *qua* rational totality and the "irrational", biological positivity of the king's body' (*E!*, 86). It is also the particular rhythm that characterizes Žižek's work: a kind of 'Schellingian' simultaneous contraction and expansion, in which proper names and concepts at once channel the disseminatory drift of the writing and argument and open it up to the loss of coherence and sense.

To return finally to that diagram with which we began, we might say that it is the very image of philosophy – or at least philosophy as seen from a Hegelian perspective. For what we see in the impossible intersection of personal description and teaching there is the attempt to make enunciation and enunciated equal in order to speak of that void or emptiness that makes the symbolic order possible. In other words, its 'doubling' of the system before (whether it be social reality or a philosophical construct) takes the place of an always excluded enunciation: it speaks of that position *from which* the equivalences of the system before are possible. And yet it could no sooner speak of this enunciation than lose it, turn it into an enunciated, allowing another to 'double' it in turn. *Object a*, that mysterious object of desire of philosophy, is just this equivalence of personal description and teaching, enunciation and enunciated, no sooner spoken of than lost, like that famous paradox, so important to Lacan, of 'I am lying' (*S*11, 138–41). And the great philosophers, those who join in this conversation, realize this, and in so doing lose it again. Philosophy is always the same story told differently, but this story is nothing but these differences. We come back to our original insight that perhaps all Žižek adds is a certain argumentative brio, a new range of references, a brilliant writerly style – in short, a new way of speaking – but all this only to stand for that nothing (*object a*) that at once completes those systems (Hegel, Lacan, contemporary capitalism) he analyses and ensures that they can never be completed. In this, he perhaps touches on the proper definition of the act as outlined in 'Why is Every Act?': he at once only repeats what is already there before him and reveals that what is does not exist before this repetition (we can only choose to enter the symbolic order and this order would not exist without us). He therefore demonstrates both that nothing is outside of the symbolic order and that we are completely undetermined by it. This is what we might call the real 'suspension' of transference at stake in philosophy: not the simple end or breaking of transference, the revealing of some original 'emptiness', but a 'suspension' that exists only in retrospect, no sooner spoken of than lost, and thus always to be taken up again. To express it formulaically: just as transference itself is only possible because of a certain breaking of transference, so this breaking of transference only exists within transference.

The reader's forced choice

How is all this to relate to what we say about Žižek here? What does all this leave us to say? Žižek on many occasions speaks about what he feels to be the overall objective of his work. It is, as we have seen in 'Why is Every Act?', to contest the naturalness and authority of every ideological construction of reality. As he says in *The Fright of Real Tears*, the aim of philosophy is not so much to argue for the reality of fictions as to make us 'experience reality itself as a fiction' (*K*, 77). Or, as he argues in the 'Introduction' to *Tarrying with the Negative*, the philosopher should attempt to 'step back' (*TN*, 2) from actuality to possibility, to show how things might be otherwise. In this, as he puts it there, they must seek to 'occupy all the time the place of the hole, i.e., to maintain a distance toward every reigning master-signifier' (*TN*, 2). And yet – to go back to the lesson of that diagram – this hole is always turning into a master-signifier; this hole can only be seen through a certain master-signifier. As Žižek states elsewhere, *object a* is the master-signifier seen 'anamorphically' (*SO*, 99; *T?*, 149). How then to maintain this distinction between *object a* and the master-signifier? How to keep 'looking awry' upon reality? It is not, as Žižek seems to be suggesting at times, a matter of an act or void *before* the master-signifier. So is *object a* merely a master-signifier in waiting? Is it a matter of keeping *object a* from turning into a master-signifier? Or must the relationship between the two be thought otherwise? Is the only way of keeping them apart to argue that they arise at the same time? That *object a* is a kind of 'possibility' born at the same time as the master-signifier? That *object a*, to use a language that Žižek will increasingly have resort to, is not so much opposed to or outside of the master-signifier as what makes the master-signifier both possible and impossible (*IR*, 144–5; *L*, 274–5)?

It is these questions that lie at the heart of this book, for, as we have already seen, one of the crucial issues at stake in any evaluation of Žižek is to what extent does he simply oppose the master-signifier and *object a* and their equivalents and to what extent does he think their relationship otherwise? It is this alternative that opens up that 'void' or 'emptiness' around which Žižek's work is organized, and that might allow us to say something 'new' about it ourselves. In Chapter 2, we take up the ideological master-signifier or quilting point as it appears in Žižek's work and see that it is neither some transcendental signified nor despotic authority that forces us to obey it, but – this is the particular problem Žižek addresses – something that as it were 'doubles' reality, that we follow whether we want to or not, that incorporates our own distance on to it. It is a distance that is to be seen not only within the master-signifier itself but in the way we relate to it – and, in both cases, it involves the *object a*. That is, if *object a* can be seen as undermining the master-signifier, imposing a certain distance on to it, it can also be understood as extending or strengthening it. The master-signifier's distance on to itself and ours on to the master-signifier paradoxically extends its reach even more, denying us any critical perspective on to it. And yet – this is the ambiguity we trace throughout here – this necessarily means that the master-signifier comes close to its own unveiling or dissolution. The very element that allows the ideological field to be sutured, that means there is no outside (that the outside is already inside), also desutures it, opens it up, ensures that there is always a certain 'distance' on to it that is necessary for it to be constituted and that can never be finally incorporated.

Accordingly, in Chapter 3, we begin the complex task of thinking *object a* as the 'opposite' or 'inverse' of the master-signifier with regard to Žižek's notion of the 'act' as that which breaks with or resituates the ideological field. But already here we might think how this act does not so much break with or resituate this field – for in that case it would be merely another master-signifier – as represent a kind of 'virtuality' or 'possibility' forever excluded from it. The act is not something that is deferred or impossible; but neither is it, as Žižek sometimes implies, something that can definitively be accomplished. Rather, it is something that is always as it were coming into being or taking place; something that, in Lacan's words, 'doesn't stop (not) being written' (*S20*, 59), without being thought of in terms of some potential becoming actual. The act, as we have seen before, is what we might call *object a* or stand-in for the Real. And, in Chapter 4, we go on to explore this notion of the act as a kind of 'virtuality' that 'doubles' every actuality, as what not only actually occurs but what allows all else to take place. That is, again, the act as *object a* is neither opposed to the master-signifier nor an inter-regnum between master-signifiers but arises *at the same time as* the master-signifier as its 'transcendental' condition of possibility. To put all this in Hegelian terms, if the master-signifier is seen as the subject of this book, in Chapter 2 we look at the master-signifier, in Chapter 3 at the 'negation' of the signifier and in Chapter 4 at the 'negation' of this 'negation' of the master-signifier (which does not simply return us to the master-signifier). Or, if *object a* is seen as the subject of this book, in Chapter 2 we look at it 'for-the-other', in Chapter 3 at it 'in-itself' and in Chapter 4 at it 'in-and-for-itself'. Finally, in Chapter 5, in an attempt to summarize these issues, we look at the various critics of Žižek (princi-pally the 'radical democrat' Ernesto Laclau and the feminist-queer theorist Judith Butler, but also briefly the Frankfurt School Marxist Peter Dews). We see raised in the arguments between them the ques-tion – the underlying subject of this book – of how to think the relation-ship between the master-signifier and the act: whether the act is outside of the symbolic and how then to name it; whether the act is within the symbolic and how then it could fundamentally change anything. What we see there is a problem we have touched on before: the difficulty of Žižek thinking the Real (or its stand-in, *object a*) as a kind of 'empty space', preceding that element which fills it in.

Our reading here – though this is not to imply any simple develop-ment in Žižek's thinking – is broadly chronological. In Chapter 2, we look extensively at *Sublime Object* and *For They Know Not*; in Chapter 3, at *Indivisible Remainder* and *Ticklish Subject*; in Chapter 4, at *Fragile Abso-lute* and *On Belief*; and, in Chapter 5, at *Contingency, Hegemony, Universal-ity*. Or, to put it another way, this time placing the emphasis not so much on what is said as its saying, we might suggest that this book divides into two contrasting approaches or tonalities. The first is what we might call, following Lacan's schema of the 'four discourses' (*CU*, 74–81), the dis-course of the 'master' or the 'university', in which, transferring on to Žižek, we seek to systematize his work, making it the source of a stable and consistent authority, explicating it as though everything had already been said by him, as though the answers to all our objections will eventually be found there. The second is what we might call the dis-course of the 'hysteric' or 'analyst', in which we seek to bring out our moments of doubt, confusion and frustration before the work, which we then attribute to Žižek himself, or in which we seek to catch him out in his shortcomings or inconsistencies. But, as we have tried to show before, these two attitudes are not strictly separable: one is always turning into the other; both are true at once. It is at that very moment when we think we see flaws in Žižek's argument that we most transfer on to him (for it is at just these moments that we feel we might one day be like him, that we are 'more in Žižek than Žižek himself'); and it is only by transferring on to Žižek that we might somehow go beyond him (it is only by completely internalizing him that we might end up saying something different from him, that we might end up becoming ourselves). Again, we come close to the secret of all significant systems of thought: at once they allow us to think – as though we could for a moment step outside of the symbolic order – that something is lost by transference, that they are not entirely saying what we think they are saying, and it is this that not only strengthens our transference on to them but leads to transference in the first place. It is not only the creators of the great philosophical systems who are split subjects in this sense, who repeat a kind of forced choice, but those who read them as well.

Chapter 2

What is a master-signifier?

Žižek begins his theoretical project in *Sublime Object* by taking up Laclau and Mouffe's notion of 'radical democracy'. As he admits in his Acknowledgements there, it is their book *Hegemony and Socialist Strategy* that first oriented him in the use of the 'Lacanian conceptual apparatus as a tool in the analysis of ideology' (*SO*, xvi). What is the essential argument of *Hegemony and Socialist Strategy?* Its fundamental insight, following the linguistics of Saussure, is that there is no necessary relationship between reality and its symbolization (*SO*, 97). Our descriptions do not naturally and immutably refer to things, but – this is the defining feature of the symbolic order – things in retrospect begin to resemble their description. Thus, in the analysis of ideology, it is not simply a matter of seeing which account of reality best matches the 'facts', with the one that is closest being the least biased and therefore the best. As soon as the facts are determined, we have already – whether we know it or not – made our choice; we are already within one ideological system or another. The real dispute has already taken place over what is to count as the facts, which facts are relevant, and so on. For example, in 1930s Germany the Nazi narrative of social reality won out over the socialist-revolutionary narrative not because it was better able to account for the 'crisis' in liberal-bourgeois ideology, but because it was able to impose the idea that there was a 'crisis' – a 'crisis' of which the socialist-revolutionary narrative was itself a part and which must ultimately be explained because of the 'Jewish conspiracy' (*TS*, 179).

The same 'arbitrariness' applies not only to reality but to those ideological systems by which we construct reality. That is, again following the analogy of Saussure's conception of language, the meaning of particular political or ideological terms is not fixed or unchanging but given only through their articulation with other terms. For example, the meaning of 'ecologism' is not the same in every ideological system but shifts between several possible meanings: there is feminist ecology, in which the exploitation of nature is seen as masculine; socialist ecology, in which the exploitation of nature is seen as the product of capitalism; conservative ecology, which urges us to get back to the cycles of nature; and even capitalist ecology, which sees the free market as the only solution to our current environmental problems (*SO*, 87). The same would apply to the terms 'feminism', 'socialism', 'conservatism' and 'capitalism' themselves. And ideology is the struggle over which of these elements not only is defined by its relationship with the others but also allows this relationship, is that medium through which they are organized. It is the struggle not only to be one of those free-floating ideological signifiers whose meaning is 'quilted' or determined by another but also that signifier which gives those others their meaning, to which they must ultimately be understood to be referring.

This is Laclau and Mouffe's project of 'radical democracy', as elaborated in *Hegemony and Socialist Strategy*.[1] But we might ask how what they propose there differs from the Marxist concept of *overdetermination*. It is a question Žižek considers at several points throughout his work (*TS*, 100–3; *CHU*, 235). And in *Sublime Object* too he takes it up. Traditional Marxism, he writes there, is defined by two presuppositions. The first is that, running beneath the various conflicts in society, there is a fundamental antagonism, which is their truth and of which they are the expression. It is *class struggle*, the economic exploitation of the workers (*SO*, 89). The second is that this assumes a time – even if it is always actually deferred – when the 'objective conditions' would allow the possibility of resolving this antagonism and ending the workers' exploitation in a totally transparent society (*SO*, 3). Laclau and Mouffe's 'anti-essentialist' approach differs from this – in so far as there is no necessary way of symbolizing reality – in that there is no single struggle that automatically comes first. As Žižek writes: 'Any of the antagonisms, which in the light of Marxism appears to be secondary, can take on the role of mediator for all the others' (*SO*, 4). And, because there is no natural, predetermined way to symbolize reality, there can be no definitive resolution of this antagonism. As opposed to some finally transparent or fully administered society, there is instead an ineradicable 'imbalance', an 'impossible-real kernel' (*SO*, 4), to which all particular struggles can be seen as a response.

But, again, why do all these attempts to 'quilt' society fail? What is this 'impossible-real kernel' that is a sign of their inability to attain closure? It is not, Žižek insists, a matter of some imaginary 'fullness' of society that is unable to be taken account of, some empirical 'richness' that is in excess of any attempt to structure it (*CHU*, 215–16). Rather, it is because whatever it is that quilts the social is itself only able to be defined, re-marked, stated as such, from somewhere outside of it. This is Laclau and Mouffe's Saussurean point that every ideological element takes on its meaning in its articulation with others. And it is this that underlies their project of 'radical democracy', why – beneath the various attempted unifications of the ideological field – society fundamentally remains open. It is because any attempt to take over this field is also an attempt to stand in for that empty signifier from which the identity of all those others can be seen; and yet, of course, as soon as we do this, we necessarily require another to see *it*. It is unable to be named as such, to transmit whatever values it represents to others, except from another point of view. This is why, as Laclau says, every hegemonic signifier aspires to a kind of ideal emptiness, as it makes more and more signifiers equivalent to it; but in the end it is unable to escape the original context from which it comes, is always able to be shown to be too 'particular' by another (*CHU*, 56–8). And what Laclau and Mouffe's 'radical democracy' marks is this paradox whereby the very success of a signifier in casting its light over others is also its failure, because it can do so only at the cost of increasingly emptying itself of any determinate meaning, or because in doing so it can always be shown not to be truly universal, to leave something out.

What this means is that, because there is no underlying society to give expression to, each master-signifier works not because it is some preexisting fullness that already contains all of the meanings attributed to it, but because it is empty, just that place from which to see the 'equivalence' of other signifiers. It is not some original reserve that holds all of its significations in advance, but only what is retrospectively recognized as what is being referred to. Thus, to take the example of 'democracy', it is not some concept common to the liberal notion of democracy, which asserts the autonomy of the individual over the state, and the socialist notion of democracy, which can only be guaranteed by a Party representing the interests of the People. It is not a proper solution to argue either that the socialist definition travesties true democracy or that the socialist alternative is the only authentic form of democracy. Rather, the only adequate way to define 'democracy' is to include all political movements and orientations that legitimate themselves by reference to 'democracy' – and which are ultimately defined only by their differential relationship to 'non-democracy'. As Žižek writes: 'The only possible definition of an object in its identity is that this is the object which is always designated by the same signifier – tied to the same signifier. It is the signifier which constitutes the kernel of the object's "identity"'

(*SO*, 98). In other words, what is crucial in any analysis of ideology is to detect, behind the apparently transcendental meaning of the element holding it together, this tautological, performative, fundamentally self-referential operation, in which it is not so much some pre-existing meaning that things refer to as an empty signifier that is retrospectively seen as what is being referred to. This ideological *point de capiton*, or master-signifier, is not some underlying unity but only the difference between elements, only what its various mentions have in common: the signifier itself as pure difference (*SO*, 99).

Laclau and Mouffe's 'radical democracy' is a recognition that ideological struggle is an attempt to 'hegemonize' the social field: to be that one element that not only is part of the social field but also quilts or gives sense to all the others – or, in Hegelian terms, to be that 'species which is its own universal kind' (*SO*, 89). But, if this is the way ideology works, it is also this contingency, the notion that the meaning of any ideological term is fundamentally empty, not given in itself but able to be interpreted in various ways, that Laclau and Mouffe argue *for*. That is, 'radical democracy' would be not only one of the actual values within the ideological field, but also that in which other values recognize themselves, that for which other values stand in. It would be not only one of the competing values within the ideological struggle, but would speak of the very grounds of this struggle. As Žižek writes:

> The dialectical paradox [of 'radical democracy'] lies in the fact that the particular struggle playing a hegemonic role, far from enforcing a violent suppression of differences, opens the very space for the relative autonomy of particular struggles: the feminist struggle, for example, is made possible only through reference to democratic-egalitarian political discourse. (*SO*, 88–9)

It is with something like this paradox that we can see Žižek grappling in his first two books. In *Sublime Object*, he thinks that it is only through the attempt to occupy the position of metalanguage that we are able to show the impossibility of doing so (*SO*, 156) and the phallus as what 'gives body to a certain fundamental loss in its very presence' (*SO*, 157). In *For They Know Not*, he thinks the king as guaranteeing the 'non-closure of the social' in so far as he is the 'place-holder of the void' (*TK*, 267) and the 'name' as what by standing in for the New is able to preserve it (*TK*, 271–3). And, in a way, Žižek will never cease this complicated gesture of thinking the void through what takes its place. In this sense, his work remains profoundly indebted to the lesson of *Hegemony and Socialist*

Strategy. But in terms of Laclau and Mouffe's specific project of 'radical democracy', Žižek's work is marked by an increasing distance taken towards it. In 'Enjoyment within the Limits of Reason Alone', his Foreword to the second edition of *For They Know Not*, he will speak of wanting to get rid of the 'remnants of the liberal-democratic stance' of his earlier thought, which 'oscillates between Marxism proper and praise of "pure" democracy' (*TK*, xviii). And, undoubtedly, Žižek's work becomes more explicitly Marxist after his first two books. But, more profoundly, this change in political orientation is linked to certain difficulties he begins to have with Laclau and Mouffe's notion of 'hegemony' itself. They might be summarized as: if political struggle is defined as the contest to put forward that master-signifier which quilts the rest of the ideological field, then what is it that keeps open that frame within which these substitutions take place? What is it that 'radical democracy' does not speak of that allows the space for their mutual contestation? As Žižek writes later in *Contingency, Hegemony, Universality*, we need to 'distinguish more explicitly between contingency/substitutability *within* a certain historical horizon and the more fundamental exclusion/foreclosure that *grounds this very horizon*' (*CHU*, 108). And this leads to Žižek's second major criticism of Laclau and Mouffe: that for all of their emphasis on the openness and contingency of signification, the way the underlying antagonism of society is never to be resolved, nothing is really contemplated happening in their work; no fundamental alteration can actually take place. There is a kind of 'resignation' in advance at the possibility of truly effecting radical change, a Kantian imperative that we cannot go too far, cannot definitively fill the void of the master-signifier, cannot know the conditions of political possibility, without losing all freedom (*CHU*, 93, 316–17).

But, again, what exactly are Žižek's objections to Laclau and Mouffe's notion of 'radical democracy'? And why is Marxism seen as the solution to them? As we have said, underlying the project of radical democracy is a recognition that society does not exist, cannot be rendered whole. It cannot be rendered whole not because of some empirical excess but because any supposed unity is only able to be guaranteed from some point outside of it, because the master-signifier that gathers together the free-floating ideological elements stands in for a void. As with the order of language, this empty signifier or signifier without signified is the way for a self-contained, synchronic system, in which the meaning of each element is given by its relationship to every other, to signify its own outside, the enigma of its origin (*TK*, 198). This means that any potential master-signifier is connected to a kind of hole or void that cannot be named, which all the elements stand in for and which is not defined by its relationship to others but is comparable only to itself: *object a*. But for Žižek, finally, Laclau and Mouffe's 'radical democracy' remains too much within a horizon simply defined *by* these elements. It does not do enough to think that frame which allows their exchangeability. More importantly, it does not do enough to *change* this frame, to bring what is excluded from it inside. It is not, in other words, that true 'concrete universality', in which the genus meets itself amongst its species in the form of its opposite (*CHU*, 99–101). For Žižek, it is not 'radical democracy' but only 'class struggle' that is able to do this, that is able to signal this antagonism – void – that sutures the various ideological elements. It is only 'class struggle' that is at once only one of the competing master-signifiers – class, race, gender – and that antagonism to which every master-signifier is an attempt to respond (*CHU*, 319–20).

Of course, at this point several questions are raised, to which we will return towards the end of this chapter and in Chapter 5. First of all, how fair are Žižek's accusations against Laclau and Mouffe when, as we have seen, radical democracy just *is* this attempt to think that 'void' that allows all requiltings, including that of 'radical democracy' itself? Is Žižek in his advocacy of 'class struggle' only continuing the principle already at stake in 'radical democracy'? Is he not with his insistence on 'class struggle' merely proposing another requilting of 'radical democracy', another renaming of the same principle? And yet, Žižek insists, it is only in this way that we can truly bring out what is at stake in 'radical democracy'. It is only in this way that we can make clear that no master-signifier is final, that every attempt to speak of the void is subject to further redefinition. It is only in this way that the process of contesting each existing master-signifier can be extended forever. (It is for this reason that Žižek will accuse Laclau in *Contingency, Hegemony, Universality* of a kind of Kantian 'formalism' (*CHU*, 111–12, 316–18), of excepting a transcendental, ahistorical space from the consequences of his own logic.) And yet, if Žižek challenges Laclau and Mouffe's 'radical democracy' on the basis of 'class', class is not exactly what he is talking about but would only stand in for it. As we have already seen, class is not to be named as such because the very effect of its presence is that it is always missed. In this sense, class is both master-signifier and *object a*, both master-signifier and what contests the master-signifier, both that void the master-signifier speaks of and that void the master-signifier covers over. Is there not therefore a similar 'resignation' or failure in Žižek, a continual falling-short of that act that would break with the symbolic and its endless substitutions? Or is this 'failure' only the symbolic itself?

Is Žižek finally not proposing an end to the symbolic but rather insisting on the necessity of thinking its 'transcendental' conditions, the taking into account of that 'outside' that makes it possible?

Accordingly, in this chapter we look at how the master-signifier works. We examine the ways in which Žižek takes it further than Laclau and Mouffe's similar notion of the hegemonic 'universal signifier'. And how he takes it further – to begin to head toward those issues we have previously signalled – is that it is not a mere extension of an existing concept tending towards emptiness, but is 'empty' from the very beginning, a pure 'doubling' of what is. That is, implicit in the idea of the master-signifier is that it is not so much an empirical observation that comes out of the world or a formal structure that precedes it as what at once makes the world over in its image and is the secret explanation of the world just as it is; something that is neither to be verified nor refuted but, as we saw in Chapter 1 with regard to class and the unconscious, is its own absence or difference from itself. And it is for this reason that later in this chapter we look at the relationship of this master-signifier to *object a* around two privileged examples in Žižek's work: the figure of the 'shark' in the film *Jaws* and the 'Jew' in anti-Semitism. In both cases, we can see that *object a* that is behind the master-signifier and that allows us to recoup its difference from itself, to say that all its variants speak of the same thing. And this will lead us to the innovative aspect of Žižek's treatment of ideology: his analysis of how a certain 'distance' – or what he calls 'enjoyment' – is necessary for its functioning. It is a distance we already find with regard to *Jaws* and Jews; but it can also be seen as a feature of ideological interpellation, as analysed by Althusser. Finally, following on from this, in the last section of this chapter, we pursue the idea that there is always a certain necessary openness by which we are able to contest any ideological closure, that the same element that sutures the ideological field also desutures it, that we are always able to find a species within it that is more universal than its genus. This again is the ambiguity of *object a* as at once what indicates that void at the origin of the symbolic constitution of society and what stands in for it. And it is this that leads us towards Chapter 3, which raises the question of *object a* as that act that would break or suspend the symbolic order of the master-signifier.

Some examples of the master-signifier

So what is a master-signifier and how does it operate in ideology? In order to answer this question, let us begin, perhaps surprisingly, with three examples taken from the realm not of politics but of art. In the chapter 'The Wanton Identity' from *For They Know Not*, in the middle of a discussion of what he calls the 're-mark', Žižek speaks of the famous third movement of the Serenade in B flat major, KV 361, by Mozart. In it, a beautiful introductory melody, played by the winds, is joined by another, played by the oboe and clarinet. At first, this second melody appears to be the accompaniment to the first, but after a while we realize that this first is in fact the accompaniment to the second, which as it were 'descends "from above"' (*TK*, 76–7). Žižek then considers the well-known 'bird's-eye' shot of Bodega Bay in flames during the attack of the birds in Hitchcock's film *The Birds*. We have what initially appears to be an unclaimed point of view, but first one bird, then another, and then another, enters the screen, until there is a whole flock hovering there before us. We soon realize that those birds, which originally appeared to be the subject of the shot, much more disquietingly provide its point of view (*TK*, 77). Finally, Žižek looks at what appears to be the reverse of this procedure, the opening scene of Francis Ford Coppola's espionage thriller, *The Conversation*. The film begins with a seemingly conventional establishing shot of workers in a square during their lunch-break, over which play random snatches of conversation. It is not until the end of the film that we realize that what we took to be mere background noise there holds the key to the plot (and to the survival of the agent who recorded it): the bugging of a furtive lunch-time liaison of an adulterous couple and their plans to murder the woman's husband (*TK*, 77).

There is a surprising turnaround in each case here – close to what a number of contemporary theorists have characterized as simulation – but we should try to explain in more detail how this 'reversal' actually occurs. In each case, we can see that it works neither by adding something to the original, proposing some complement to it, nor by inverting the original, suggesting some alternative to it. In Mozart, that second melodic line is not a variation upon or even the counterpoint to the first. In *The Birds*, we never see whose point of view the 'bird's-eye' shot represents. In *The Conversation*, no one is sure until the end of the film what the significance of the conversation is. The 're-mark' does not so much 'add' as 'subtract' something – or, more subtly, we might say that it adds a certain 'nothing'. What the addition of that second, 're-marking' element reveals is that something is missing from the first, that what was originally given is incomplete. That order we initially took to be self-evident, 'unre-marked', is shown to be possible only because of another. That place from which the world is seen is reflected back into the world – and the world cannot be realized without it

(*TK*, 13). Or, to put this another way, the world is understood not merely to *be* but to *signify*, to belong to a symbolic economy, to be something whose presence can only be grasped against the potential absence or background of another (*TK*, 22).

Thus, to return to our examples, the genius of Mozart in the third movement of the Serenade is not that the second motif retrospectively converts the first into a variant of it, but that it suggests that *both* are ultimately variants of another, not yet given, theme. It reveals that the notes that make up the first are precisely *not* other notes, for example, but only, for example, those of the second. This is the 'divine' aspect of Mozart's music: it is able to imply that *any* given musical motif only stands in for another, as yet unheard, one that is greater than anything we could imagine. And this is the genius of Hitchcock too in *The Birds* (of which *The Conversation* is an aural variant), for in that Bodega Bay sequence the ultimate point of view is not that of the birds but that of off-screen space itself, for which the birds are only substitutes. Indeed, the French film theorist Pascal Bonitzer speaks of this 'doubling' or 're-marking' of what is in terms of the 'gaze' in the essay 'Hitchcockian Suspense' he writes for the Žižek-edited collection *Everything You Always Wanted to Know*. He begins by conjuring up that archetypal scene from early cinema, in which we see a young nanny pushing a pram being courted by an amorous soldier in a park. He then speaks of the way that, signalled by an intervening crime, what at first seemed innocent and sentimental becomes: 'Troubled, doubled, distorted and "hollowed out" by a second signification, which is cruel and casts back every gesture on to a face marked by derision and the spirit of the comic and macabre, which brings out the hidden face of simple gestures, the face of nothingness' (*H*, 20). That is, the soldier and the nanny can now be seen to be playing a dangerous and ambiguous game: the nanny wishing to drown the baby; the soldier dreaming of assaulting the nanny. But, again, the crucial aspect here is that none of this actually has to happen, nor does the crime even have to take place. The peculiar form of Hitchcockian 'suspense' lies in what is left *out* of the scene, what does *not* happen; this other place or possibility – which we might call the 'death's-head' (*H*, 20) of the gaze – for which what we do see stands in.

It is this reversal of meaning that we also have in Žižek's other examples of the master-signifier in *For They Know Not*, which is that book of his where he deals most extensively, as he says, 'on the One' (*TK*, 7–60). The first is the notorious Dreyfus Affair, which in 1898 saw an innocent Jewish captain of the French Army, Alfred Dreyfus, sent to Devil's Island for being part of a plot to overthrow the government of the day.

It is an episode that even now has its effects: the separation of Church and state in modern democracies, socialist collaboration in reformist governments, the birth of both Zionism and right-wing populist political movements. The decisive incident of the whole affair, argues Žižek, did not occur when we might at first think, during that moment when Dreyfus was initially accused and then vigorously defended by the writer Zola, when the facts were weighed up and appeals made to the rule of law. Rather, the turning-point came later, when all was seemingly lost for the anti-Dreyfus forces, when the evidence seemed most stacked against them. It was the episode in which the Chief of French Intelligence, Lieutenant Colonel Henry, who had just been arrested for forging documents implicating Dreyfus, committed suicide in his cell. Of course, to an unbiased observer, this could not but look like an admission of guilt. Nevertheless, it was at this point that the decisive intervention occurred. It was that of the little-known journalist Charles Maurras who, outwitting his better credentialled opponents, argued that this action by Henry was not evidence *against* the plot in which Dreyfus was implicated but evidence *for* it. That is, looked at in the right way – and here the connection with Hitchcock's notion of the 'gaze' – Henry's forgery and suicide were not an admission of guilt but, on the contrary, the heroic actions of a man who, knowing the judiciary and press were corrupt, made a last desperate attempt to get his message out to the people in a way they could not prevent. As Žižek says of Maurras's masterstroke: 'It looked at things in a way no one had thought or dared to look' (*TK*, 28) – and, we might even say, what Maurras added, like Hitchcock, is just this look itself; what he makes us see is that Henry's actions were meant *for* our look and cannot be explained outside of it.

We find the same sudden reversal of meaning – the same turning of defeat into victory – in our next example from *For They Know Not*. It is that of St Paul, the founder of the Christian Church. How is it, we might ask, that St Paul was able to 'institutionalize' Christianity, give it its 'definitive contours' (*TK*, 78), when so many others had tried and failed before him? What is it that he did to ensure that Christ's Word endured, would not be lost and in a way *could* not be lost? As Žižek writes, in a passage that should remind us of what we said in our Introduction about how the messages of our great philosophers cannot be superseded or distorted:

> He [St Paul] did not add any new content to the already-existing dogmas – all he did was to re-mark as the greatest triumph, as the fulfilment of Christ's supreme mission (reconciliation of God with

mankind), what was before experienced as traumatic loss (the defeat of Christ's mundane mission, his infamous death on the cross) ... 'Reconciliation' does not convey any kind of miraculous healing of the wound of scission; it consists solely in a reversal of perspective by means of which we perceive how the scission is already in itself reconciliation. To accomplish 'reconciliation' we do not have to 'overcome' the scission, we just have to re-mark it. (*TK*, 78)

We might say that, if St Paul discovers or institutes the word of Christ here, it is in its properly symbolic sense. For what he brings about is a situation in which the arguments used *against* Christ (the failure of His mission, His miserable death on the cross) are now reasons *for* Him (the sign of His love and sacrifice for us). Again, as opposed to the many competing prophets of the time, who sought to adduce evidence of miracles, and so on, it is no extra dimension that St Paul provides (that in fact Christ succeeded here on earth, proof of the afterlife). Rather, he shows that our very ability to take account of these defeats already implies a kind of miracle, already is a kind of miracle. Defeat here, as understood through the mediation of Christ's love, is precisely not a sign of a victory to come but already a form of victory. St Paul *doubles* what is through the addition of an empty signifier – Christ's worldly mission – so that henceforth the very lack of success *is* success, the failure of proof *is* proof. Through this 're-mark', the very fact that this defeat is seen means that it is intended to be seen, that a lesson or strength is sought to be gained from it. This gaze on to events becomes part of these events themselves. It is what Lacan in his Seminar on *Ethics* calls the 'point of view of the Last Judgement' (*S7*, 294). And in this would lie the 'superiority' of Christianity over both atheism (St Paul) and Jewishness (Maurras). Exactly like the figure of the king for Hegel, through Christ we are able to bring together the highest and the lowest, the Son of God and the poorest and most abject of men (*TK*, 85). Indeed, this is what Hegel means by dialectical sublation – or this is what allows dialectical sublation – not the gradual coming-together of two things, but a kind of immediate doubling and reversal of a thing into its opposite. Seen from another hitherto excluded perspective, the one already *is* the other, already is 'reconciled' to the other (although, as we have seen, it is also this that allows us to think their separation, what cannot be taken up or sublated).

We might just offer here one more example of this kind of 'conversion' from *For They Know Not*, which originally derives from Lacan's Seminar on *The Psychoses*. It is another instance, like St Paul, of the symbolic power of speech, or what Lacan calls 'full speech'; but it is a 'full speech', paradoxically – and here again we return to the lesson of our great philosophers – that is 'full' in being 'empty'. (Or, more accurately, it is a speech that is able to bring about the effect of imaginary misrecognition, of always referring to present circumstances, through its symbolic ability to turn failure into success. That is, as Žižek insists in *For They Know Not*, the Imaginary and the Symbolic are not two opposed registers, for within the Imaginary itself there is always a point of 'double reflection' [*TK*, 10], where the Imaginary is hooked on to the Symbolic.)[2] It is exactly in saying 'nothing' that the word lives on, is transmitted. This last example is from the play *Athalie* by Racine – and it too involves a certain 'plot'. The master-signifier this time is to be found in the words of one of the play's characters, the high priest Jehoiada, to the recent convert Abner who, despite his brave actions, still fears what is being done to the Christians under King Athaliah and is unsure as to the ultimate outcome of their struggle. In response to Abner's doubts, Jehoiada replies:

> The one who puts a stop to the fury of the waves
> Knows also of the evil men how to stop the plots.
> Subservient with respect to his holy will,
> I fear God, dear Abner, and have no other fear. (*TK*, 16)

As Žižek emphasizes, faced with the anxiety and uncertainty of Abner, who in fact is always waiting to be discouraged, Jehoiada does not attempt logically to persuade him. He does not argue that Christianity is winning or promise him heaven (both of which, as it were, would be only the *consequence* of belief and not its *explanation*). Rather, he simply states that all of these earthly fears and hopes are as nothing compared to the fear of God Himself. Suddenly – and, again, it is the notion of 'conversion' that Žižek is playing on – all of these worldly concerns are seen in a different light. What allows religious conversion is not the prospect of imminent success on earth or the future promise of heaven, but the fear of God Himself, by comparison to which the worst here is *already* like being in heaven. (At the same time – and this is why Žižek is able to repeat Feuerbach's critique of religion as offering a merely specular, reversed image of the world, secretly determined by what it opposes [*TK*, 17] – it is through this impossible, virtual space that we would be able to mark the failure of *any* actual heaven to live up to its ideal, that we can know that *any* heaven we can actually grasp is not yet it.) It is only at this point that the proper gesture of 'quilting' or *point de capiton* takes place. Abner is transformed from an uncontrolled zealot, whose fervour marks a deep insecurity, to a true and faithful adherent, who is convinced of his mission and who neither needs the reward of heaven nor is shaken by events that appear to go against him.

This is, indeed, the suddenness or immediacy of symbolic conversion, as emphasized by Žižek (and intimated in various ways by St Paul and Hegel). It does not properly work by reason, argument, persuasion. It can never be grasped as such. We are always too late to catch it in action because it has already erased itself, made it seem as though it is merely describing things as they are. Any evidence or confirmation would remain only at the level of the Imaginary, always in the form of horoscopes, predictions, self-fulfilling prophecies. And, equally, it is not even a matter of subjective belief, as all the great theologians already knew. The Word, the Other, already believes for us, and we can only follow. There is always a belief before belief. Self-knowledge and self-reflection come about only afterwards. And all of this is why, if St Paul is able to found an institution on the Word of God, he also cannot, because there is always something about the master-signifier that resists being fixed in this way. *But this is what God, this is what the institution, this is what the master-signifier, is.* The master-signifier is the name for its own difference from itself. The master-signifier names its own difference from itself. And to go back to Lacan's Seminar on *The Psychoses*, in which he first begins to formulate his theory of the master-signifier, this is just what the psychotic is unable to do. As Lacan comments there, a little psychosis, as seen in something like paranoia, is normal: the constitution of a coherent symbolic reality requires a certain reading in of plots, of hidden meanings, behind the apparent surface of things. And, of course, what this suggests is the possibility of another plot behind this plot, and so on. But what the psychotic is unable to do is stop at a certain point and say that this infinite regress *is* what the plot is: the symbolic closure of the Name-of-the-Father or master-signifier has been foreclosed to them.[3] It is in this regard that the Church is necessarily in touch with something that goes beyond it, a sort of performative miracle outside of any institutionalization, which at once opens up and closes down the difference of the master-signifier from itself: *object a*. As Lacan notes admiringly of Christianity and its *point de capiton*: 'You will say to me – That really is a curate's egg! Well, you're wrong. The curates have invented absolutely nothing in this genre. To invent a thing like this you have to be a poet or a prophet' (*S3*, 267).

Jaws and Jews

But, despite all we have said so far, we have not perhaps spoken enough about the master-signifier. Are not the examples we have given far-fetched, not typical of the way contemporary society actually operates? Do we really see such conspiracies as the Dreyfus case any more? Can a situation suddenly be 'converted' and turned around, as in St Paul and *Athalie*? Do such *points de capiton* as the 'Jewish plot' and the 'fear of God' truly exist in today's world? Is there a single 'quilting' point that is effectively able to condense an entire ideological field and make us see it in its terms? And, along these lines, how are we to obtain any critical distance on to the master-signifier? How are we to speak of its failure when it is just this 'failure' that the master-signifier already takes into account, that the master-signifier *is*? How to oppose anything to the master-signifier when one of the first things affected by it is the 'very standard by means of which we measure alienation' (*TK*, 15)? How to step outside of this ideological space when the very idea of some non-ideological space is the most ideological illusion of all (*MI*, 19–20)? And what of the role of *object a* in all of this, as what allows this differential structure according to which the master-signifier is defined by what it is not, in which the outside is inside (extra-ideological space is ideological) and the inside is outside (the symbolic order works only in so far as there is some distance on to it)? How does *object a* function to ensure that there is no outside to the symbolic order, but only in so far as there is a certain 'outside' to it?

In order to answer these questions, let us begin by taking up undoubtedly Žižek's best-known example of the master-signifier in action: the figure of the shark from *Jaws*. Of course, like all great movie monsters, the shark can be seen as representative of many things, from the forces of nature fighting back (as humans increasingly encroach on its territory), to the eruption of sexuality (it appears after two teenagers attempt to have sex in the water), from the threat of the Third World to America (the shark, like illegal immigrants, arrives by the sea) to the excesses of capitalism (as revenge for the greed of the town mayor and resort owners in refusing to close the beach during a holiday weekend). In this sense, the shark can be understood as allowing the expression of ordinarily repressed desires and impulses within society, making explicit its usually unspoken ideologies and beliefs. And it is into this interpretive milieu that the analyst enters when they argue that it is their conception of the shark that best offers an insight into the society that produced it. However, as we have already seen with the 'rise' of the Nazi narrative in Germany in the 1930s, it is exactly here *not* a matter of deciding which account of the shark best corresponds to the truth of contemporary society, for it is the shark itself that each time constructs society in its image. Or, to put it another way, the analyst already has something to say about society (some point to make about the environment, sexuality or capitalism), which they then attribute to the shark. In both cases, what is not questioned – what the overwhelming physical presence of the shark allows us to forget – is that this is only an *interpretation* of society. What is not seen is that circularity according to which the shark is seen as embodying certain tendencies that have already been attributed to the shark. As Žižek says of what he calls this 'direct content analysis': '[It] proceeds too quickly and presupposes as self-evident the fantasy surface itself, the empty form/frame which offers space for the appearance of the monstrous content' (*E!*, 133).

That is, the true ideological effect of the shark, how it functions as a master-signifier, is to be found not in the way it represents certain tendencies in society that are already recognized but in the way it allows us to perceive and state these tendencies for the first time. It is the shark itself that allows the various fantasies and desires of the analyst – the true 'monstrous content' Žižek speaks of – to be expressed as though with some evidence, as though speaking of something that is actually there. As we saw with the re-mark, if the shark appears merely the expression of social forces that already exist, these forces would also not exist without the shark. If the shark appears simply to put a name to things, these things could also not be perceived before being named. (Žižek says the same thing about Hitchcock's *The Birds*: that if the film dramatizes certain pre-existing family tensions, these tensions could not be seen without the birds ([*LA*, 104–6]).[4] But, again – this is the very 'fantasy frame' that allows these 'monstrous contents' to be registered – in this circularity something new is brought about. If the shark expresses only what is already attributed to it by various interpreters, it also appears to be what they are all talking about, what they all have in common, even in their very differences from and disagreements with each other. It is over the meaning of the *shark* that they dispute, as though it is real, as though it is more than others see in it. And it is in this way, finally, that the shark acts as a master-signifier, as what various ideological tendencies recognize themselves in, what 'quilts' them, makes them equivalent. As the critic Fredric Jameson writes, in a passage cited by Žižek:

> The vocation of the symbol – the killer shark – lies less in any single message or meaning than in its very capacity to absorb and organize all of these quite distinct anxieties together. As a symbolic vehicle,

then, the shark must be understood more in terms of its essentially
polysemous function rather than as any particular content
attributable to it by this or that spectator. (*E!*, 133)

However, to try to draw out what Jameson is saying a little more,
what is implied here is that there is some 'real' shark behind all of the
various interpretations of it. It would be a shark that is not only what is
in common to all of these interpretations but what all of them try (and
fail) to take account of. It would be a shark that is more than any of these
interpretations and that is unable to be captured by any one of them –
something that in a sense cannot be named, and for which the shark itself
is only a substitute (*TN*, 149).[5] It is what Žižek calls in similar circumstances what is 'in shark more than shark', the shark as *object a*. And it is
what we have already seen makes it so hard to think outside of the
master-signifier, because this outside is what the master-signifier is.
From now on, the very differences or even incommensurabilities in
interpretation (of society) are only able to take place as though they are
arguing over the 'same' shark. But let us try to analyse how this *object a*
works to allow the master-signifier, and how, if it closes off any simple
outside, it might also open up a certain 'alternative' to it. As we say, the
shark is merely a tissue of differences. In a circular way, it is not what
various interpretations seek to describe but what is retrospectively seen
to fill out various interpretations. To this extent, there is a kind of infinite
regress implied in trying to speak the truth of the various interpretations
of the shark in so far as they correspond to the social, because this social
can only be seen through the shark. As with the system of language, the
shark and these various interpretations of the social are mutually defining. And yet, as with the system of language, we must also try to find
what all of these elements attempt to stand in for, what initiates this process of definition. And this is what Žižek calls the shark as *object a*: what
holds the place of that 'pure difference' (*SO*, 99) that both the shark and
its interpretations seek to exchange themselves for.

We might put this another way – and begin to think what Žižek
means when he says that ideology today already incorporates its own
distance from itself. We have spoken of how the shark is never a neutral
or natural object but always from the beginning only a reflection or
expression of competing ideologies. And it is into this contested field
that the analyst necessarily enters. That is, even the first description of
the shark is already an attempt to speak of, displace, other interpretations. Each description is not merely a description but as it were a
metadescription, an attempt to provide that *point de capiton* that quilts all the

others. Thus, when it speaks of the shark, it also wants to speak of what all those others that speak of it have in common, what they all stand in for. And it is in this sense – it is just this that we see in cultural studies-style analyses of such objects as *Jaws* – that each attempt not only is ideological but also attempts to break with ideology, to take a certain distance from those other accounts which it perceives as ideological, to speak of what they leave out. But it is precisely in this way that the shark once again weaves its magic, for we are only able to criticize others for being ideological by assuming that there *is* some real shark that others – and perhaps, in a final 'postmodern' twist, even we – get wrong. That is, in order to criticize others for being ideological, for seeing the shark only as a reflection of their own interests, we have to assume a 'true' shark that they do not speak of, which can only be a reflection of us. As Žižek writes: 'This tension introduces a kind of reflective distance into the very heart of ideology: ideology is always, by definition, "ideology of ideology" … There is no ideology that does not assert itself by means of delimiting itself from another mere "ideology"' (*MI*, 19).

To be more exact, what each master-signifier attempts to speak of is that difference – that gap or void in the signifying order – that allows others (and even itself) to speak of it. In a paradoxical way, at once each master-signifier begins by attempting to displace the others, to speak of that difference excluded to allow any of them to speak of the others, and this difference would not exist until after *it*. This, again, is Žižek's insight that the shark as master-signifier does not precede the various attempts to speak of it, but is only the after-effect of the failure to do so, is nothing but the series of these failures. However, it is just this that provokes a kind of infinite regress, with a certain lack – *object a* – always to be made up, as each successive master-signifier attempts to speak of what precedes and allows the one before. And in this context the anti-ideological gesture *par excellence* is not at all to speak of what is left out of each master-signifier, of how it 'distorts' reality, but to show how it structurally takes the place of a certain void, is merely 'difference perceived as identity' (*SO*, 99). But, again, this is very complex – and we return to those questions we raised in Chapter 1 – in that this attempt to speak of that void that precedes and makes possible the master-signifier can only be another master-signifier. In that ambiguity that runs throughout this book, that *object a* we speak of that allows this differential structure of the master-signifier, as what all of these differences have in common, at once is the only way we have of exposing the master-signifier and is only another master-signifier, reveals the emptiness that precedes the master-signifier and can do this only by filling it up again.

All of this points towards the very real difficulties involved in the analysis of ideology – not only, as Žižek often indicates, in so-called 'discourse analysis', whose presumption of a non-ideological space can always be shown to be ideological, but even in Žižek's own project of uncovering the 'sublime object' or *object a* of ideology. But in order to consider this in more detail, let us turn to perhaps the privileged example of the master-signifier (and of *object a*) in Žižek's work: the anti-Semitic figure of the 'Jew'. We have already, of course, looked at the notion of the 'Jewish plot' with regard to the Dreyfus case. It is the idea that, behind the seemingly innocent surface of things, events are secretly being manipulated by a conspiracy of Jews. More specifically, as we see for instance in Nazism, it is the idea that the series of different reasons for Germany's decline in the 1930s, reasons that would require detailed social and historical – that is, political – analysis, are ultimately to be explained by the presence of Jews. And yet, as with the shark in *Jaws*, it is not as though these 'Jews' embody any actual qualities, correspond to any empirical reality; or they are only to be defined by their very 'polysemousness', their contradictoriness – as Žižek says, Jews are understood to be both upper *and* lower class, intellectual *and* dirty, impotent *and* highly sexed (*SO*, 125). This is why the anti-Semite is not to be discouraged by the lack of empirical evidence, the appeal to facts, the way that Jews are not really as they describe them. The notion of the 'Jewish plot', like all of our master-signifiers, functions not directly but only indirectly, incorporates our very disbelief or scepticism into it. It is for this reason, as Žižek writes, that even when confronted with evidence of the 'ordinariness' of his archetypal Jewish neighbour, Mr Stern, the anti-Semite does not renounce their prejudices but, on the contrary, only finds in this further confirmation of them: ' "You see how dangerous they really are? It is difficult to recognize their true nature. They hide it behind the mask of everyday appearance – and it is exactly this hiding of one's real nature, this duplicity, that is a basic feature of the Jewish nature" ' (*SO*, 49). And this is why, behind the obvious conspiracy – that of the master-signifier – there needs to be another, of which the master-signifier itself is part. As Žižek writes in the essay 'Between Symbolic Fiction and Fantasmatic Spectre: Towards a Lacanian Theory of Ideology':

> This other, hidden law acts the part of the 'Other of the Other' in the Lacanian sense, the part of the meta-guarantee of the consistency of the big Other (the symbolic order that regulates social life). The 'conspiracy theory' provides a guarantee that the field of the big

Other is not an inconsistent bricolage: its basic premise is that, behind the public Master (who, of course, is an imposter), there is a hidden Master, who effectively keeps everything under control. ('BS', 50)

But what exactly is wrong with the empirical refutation of anti-Semitism? Why do we have the feeling that it does not effectively oppose its logic, and in a way even repeats it (just as earlier we saw the cultural studies-style rejection of competing interpretations of the shark – 'It is not really like that!' – far from breaking our fascination with the shark, in fact continuing or even constituting it)? Why are we always too late with regard to the master-signifier, only able to play its interpretation against the object or the object against its interpretation, when it is the very circularity between them that we should be trying to grasp? Undoubtedly, Žižek's most detailed attempt to describe how the master-signifier works with regard to the Jew is the chapter 'Does the Subject Have a Cause?' in *Metastases of Enjoyment*. As he outlines it there, in a first moment in the construction of anti-Semitic ideology, a series of markers that apparently speak of certain 'real' qualities is seen to designate the Jew, or the Jew appears as a signifier summarizing – Žižek's term is 'immediating, abbreviating' – a cluster of supposedly effective properties. Thus:

(1) (avaricious, profiteering, plotting, dirty ...) is *called* Jewish.

Then, in a second moment, we reverse this process and 'explicate' the Jew with the same series of qualities. Thus:

(2) X is called Jewish *because they are* (avaricious, profiteering, plotting, dirty ...).

Finally, we reverse the order again and posit the Jew as what Žižek calls the 'reflexive abbreviation' of the entire series. Thus:

(3) X is (avaricious, profiteering, plotting, dirty ...) *because they are* Jewish (*ME*, 48–9).

In this third and final stage, as Žižek says, Jew 'explicates' the very preceding series it 'immediates' or 'abbreviates'. In it, 'abbreviation and explication dialectically coincide' (*ME*, 48). That is, within the discursive space of anti-Semitism, Jews are not simply Jews because they display that set of qualities (profiteering, plotting . . .) previously attributed to them. Rather, they have this set of qualities *because they are Jewish.* What is the difference? As Žižek emphasizes, even though stage (3) appears tautological, or seems merely to confirm the circularity between (1) and (2), this is not true at all. For what is produced by this circularity is a certain supplement 'X', what is 'in Jew more than Jew': Jew not just as master-signifier but as *object a.* As Žižek says, with stage (3) we are not just thrown back on to our original starting-point, for now Jew is 'no longer a simple abbreviation that designates a series of markers but the name of the hidden ground of this series of markers that act as so many expression-effects of this ground' (*ME*, 49). Jew is not merely a series of qualities, but what these qualities stand in for. Jew is no longer a series of differences, but different even from itself. But, again, what exactly is meant by this? How is the Jew able to move from a series of specific qualities, no matter how diverse or even contradictory, to a master-signifier covering the *entire* ideological field without exception? How is it that we are able to pass, to use an analogy with Marx's analysis of the commodity form that Žižek often plays on, from an expanded to a 'general' or even 'universal' form of anti-Semitism (*ME*, 49)?

The first thing to note here is that stages (1) and (2) are not simply symmetrical opposites. In (1), corresponding perhaps to that first moment of ideological critique we looked at with *Jaws*, a number of qualities are attributed to the Jew in an apparently immediate, unreflexive way: (profiteering, plotting . . .) is Jew. In (2), corresponding to that second moment of ideological critique, these same qualities are then attributed to the Jew in a mediated, reflexive fashion: Jew is (profiteering, plotting . . .). In other words, as with the shark in *Jaws*, we do not so much speak directly about the Jew but about others' attempts to speak of the Jew. Each description before all else seeks to dispute, displace, contest others' attempts to speak of the Jew. Each description is revealed as a meta-description, an attempt to say what the Jew and all those others have in common. Each description in (1) is revealed to be an implicit explication in (2). Each attempts to name that difference – that 'Jew' – that is left out by others' attempts to speak of the Jew. Each attempts to be the master-signifier of the others. And yet – this is how (3) 'returns' us to (1); this is how the Jew is not just a master-signifier but also an *object a* – to the very extent that the Jew is only the relationship between discourses, what allows us to speak of others' relationship to the Jew, there is always necessarily another that comes after *us* that speaks of *our* relationship to the Jew. Jew in this sense is that 'difference' behind any attempt to speak of difference, that 'conspiracy' behind any

named conspiracy. That is, each description of the Jew can be understood as the very failure to adopt a metaposition *vis-à-vis* the Jew. Each
attempt to take up a metaposition in (2) is revealed to be merely another
in an endless series of qualities in (1). That master-signifier in (2) that
tries to name what all these different descriptions have in common fails
precisely because we *can* always name another; the series is always open
to that difference that allows it to be named. And 'Jew', we might say, is
the name for this very difference itself: *object a*.

We might put this another way in thinking how we finally get to the
master-signifier in its 'universal' form, the master-signifier as where
'abbreviation and explication dialectically coincide'. As we have
already said, each description of the master-signifier is before all else an
attempt to stand in for the other, to take the place of that void which the
Jew and its previous descriptions have in common. And yet each description necessarily fails. For any attempt to say what a Jew is we can always
find an exception; we can always be accused once again of leaving out
the Jew. Indeed, in a certain way, our own list is made up of *nothing
but exceptions*, attempts to say what those previous descriptions left out.
We ultimately have only an endless series of predicates with nothing in
common or, as Žižek says, a 'never-ending series of "equivalences", of
signifiers which represent for it [the master-signifier] the void of its
inscription' (*TK*, 23). Nevertheless, as we say, each new predicate, if it
attempts to stand in for this void, also opens it up again. It too will
require another to say what *it* and all those others have in common.
As before, we can never finally say what all those descriptions share,
what is behind them all. There is no way of saying what a Jew is or even
how this sequence began in the first place. The only way out of this
impasse – this, again, is how the master-signifier comes to be supplemented by *object a* – is to reverse this, so that the Jew just *is* this difference, the void of its inscription, what allows us to speak of the failure to
symbolize the Jew. As Žižek says, the only way out is to 'reverse the series
of equivalences and ascribe to one signifier the function of representing
the object (the place of inscription) for all the others (which thereby
become "all", that is, are totalized). In this way, the proper master-
signifier is produced' (*TK*, 23).

However, to put all of this in a more Hegelian perspective – in which
scission is already reconciliation – it is not as though this reversal actually has to take place. Rather, our very ability to mark these attempted
descriptions as failures, as exceptions, that is, our very ability to re-mark
them at all (close to the idea that there is not a 'crisis' until the narrative
of Nazism or that those various ideological forces cannot be articulated

until the arrival of the shark), already indicates that they stand in for an absent signifier. We cannot even have this endless series of predicates unless they are all speaking about the 'same' Jew. If we can never say what the Jew is, then this is only because, as Žižek says of the letter (*SO*, 160) – and the Jew *is* only a letter or a signifier (*TN*, 150)— we have already found it. The Jew is nothing else but this endless series of predicates, this perpetual difference from itself. Crucially, however, if the Jew cannot be made into a 'figure' (named as such), neither can it be designated a 'ground' (that for which things stand in). For, in that way we have just seen, *any* attempt to say what a Jew is, even as a series of qualities, is only to open up an exception, raise the necessity for another ground against which *this* can be seen. Rather, the 'Jew' as *object a*, the 'sublime object' of ideology, is what allows (and disallows) the relationship between ground and figure, is that void for which both stand in. If in one way, that is, the Jew can only be seen as either (1) or (2), figure or ground, in another way, as we have seen with the shark, it is the very circularity between them. And in speaking of the Jew as the 'dialectical coincidence' of 'abbreviation' (figure) and 'explication' (ground), Žižek does not mean that they become the same or are ever finally reconciled, but that each exchanges itself for the other, holds the place of the other. The description of the empirical Jew in (1) is only possible because of the underlying Jew of (2). And every attempt to say what the Jew as master-signifier is in (2) fails, reveals itself only to be the Jew of (1). (1) is only possible because of (2) and (2) can only be seen as (1), but this only because of the Jew of (3), the Jew not only as the various signifiers of (2), what they all have in common, but the very difference between them, what they all stand in for. It is Jew as the name for this difference, as what is always different from itself. It is Jew not only as present in its absence but absent in its presence, as what *everything*, including any named Jew, tries and fails to represent: the Jew as truly 'universal'.[6]

Identification with the master-signifier

We see the same thing in terms of how we *identify* with the master-signifier. Just as Žižek shows the necessity of something outside of the symbolic order (*object a*) for the constitution of the master-signifier, so he will show the necessity of something outside of meaning (what he will call 'enjoyment') for ideological identification to occur. It is by means of this 'enjoyment' that ideology can take its failure into account in advance, that deliberate ignorance or cynicism (pre- or post-ideology) is not outside of ideology but is the very form it takes today. And it is by theorizing this 'self-reflexive' aspect of ideology, the way it is able to incorporate its own distance from itself, that Žižek has been able to revivify and extend the traditional categories of ideology-critique. But a complex question is raised at this point, close to the one Žižek puts to Laclau in *Contingency, Hegemony, Universality*: is what is being described here a new, postmodern variant upon ideological iden-tification, or has it always been the case? Is this addition of what appears to be 'beyond ideology' only what is required for it to work in a time of widespread disbelief, or has it always been necessary? And another series of questions is further suggested: if this 'distance' returns us to ideology, is part of its operation, might it not also offer a certain admission by ideology of its weakness? Might not this 'distance', if it closes off any simple alternative to ideology, also open up an internal limit on to it, the fact that it can operate only through this 'outside'? And would this not point to – to use a 'feminine' logic we will return to throughout what follows – not an exception allowing a universal but the ambiguity of the *entire system* of ideology, in which every element at once reveals and attempts to cover over this 'outside'?

Žižek's most extensive explanation of ideological identification is to be found in the chapter 'Che Vuoi?' of *Sublime Object*. He offers there a three-part account of the workings of ideology that in many regards corresponds to the three stages in the constitution of the master-signifier. In a first, instinctive conception of identification, we see it as taking place on the level of the Imaginary, in which we identify with the *image* of the Other. It is an image in which 'we appear likeable to our-selves, with the image repeating "what we would like to be" ' (*SO*, 105). It is an image that we feel potentially reflects us: movie stars, popular heroes, great intellectuals and artists. However, as Žižek emphasizes, not only is this not factually true – we often identify with less-than-appealing characters – but this imaginary identification cannot be grasped outside of symbolic identification. In symbolic identification, we identify not with the *image* but with the *look* of the Other, not with how we see ourselves *in them* but with how we are seen *by them*. We see ourselves through the way that others see us. We do not identify directly with ourselves but only through another. Žižek provides an example of this in *Sublime Object* when he speaks of religious belief. Here we do not believe directly but only because others do. We do not believe ourselves, but others believe for us. As Žižek writes: 'When we subject ourselves to the machine of a religious [we might also say social] ritual, we already believe without knowing it; our belief is already materialized in the external ritual; in other words, we already believe *unconsciously*' (*SO*, 43). We find another example of this symbolic identification in Woody Allen's film *Play it Again, Sam*, in which a neurotic and insecure intellectual (played by Allen) learns life lessons from a fictitious Bogart figure, who visits him from time to time. At the end of the film, in a replay of the famous last scene of *Casablanca*, after an affair with his best friend's wife, Allen meets her at an airport late at night and renounces her, thus allowing her to leave with her husband. When his lover says of his speech: 'It's beautiful', he replies: 'It's from *Casablanca*. I've waited my whole life to say it.' And it is at this point that the Bogart figure appears for the last time, saying that, by giving up a woman for a friend, he has '"finally got some class" and no longer needs him' (*SO*, 109). Now, the first point to realize here is that the Allen character is not so much speaking to the woman in this final scene as to Bogart. He is not acting selflessly in forsaking her but in order to impress Bogart. That is, he does not identify with Bogart on the Imaginary level – with whatever qualities he possesses – but with the symbolic position he occupies. He attempts to see himself from where he sees Bogart. As Žižek writes: 'The hero realizes his identification by enacting in reality Bogart's role from *Casablanca* – by assuming a certain "mandate", by occupying a certain place in the intersubjective symbolic network' (*SO*, 110). More precisely, he identifies with Bogart's seeming position *outside* of the symbolic order. It is his apparent *difference* from other people that changes everything about him and converts those qualities that would otherwise be unattractive into something unique and desirable. It is just this that we see at the end of the film, when Allen has his last conversation with Bogart, telling him that he no longer needs him in so far as he has become like him: ' "True, you're not too tall and kind of ugly but what the hell, I'm short enough and ugly enough to succeed on my own" ' (*SO*, 110).

However, this Symbolic is still not the final level of identification. Like every other master-signifier (freedom, democracy, the environment), Bogart always falls short, proves disappointing, fails to live up to his promise. As a result, we are forced to step in, take his place, complete what he is unable to. (It is this that we see at the end of the film when the Allen character says that he no longer needs Bogart.) And yet this is not at all to break with transference but is its final effect. (It is just when Allen is most 'himself' that he is most like Bogart.) As we have already seen in 'Why is Every Act?', it is not simply a matter of identifying with some quality or gaze of the Other as though they are aware of it. Rather, the full effect of transference comes about through an identification with something that the Other does *not* appear aware of, that seems specifically meant for us, that comes about only because of us. To use the language of the previous section, we do not so much identify with the Other as holder of the Symbolic (as differentially defined from others, as master-signifier) as with what is in the Other 'more than themselves' (with what is different from itself, *object a*). If in the Imaginary we identify with the *image* of the Other, and in the Symbolic with the *look* of the Other, here in this final level we return almost to our original *look upon* the Other. Or it is perhaps the very undecidability as to whether the Other is looking at us or not that captivates us and makes us want to take their place.

To put this another way, because symbolic authority is arbitrary, performative, not to be accounted for by any 'real' qualities in its possessor, the subject when appealed to by the Other is always unsure (*SO*, 113). They are unsure whether this is what the Other really does want of them, whether this truly is the desire of the Other. And they are unsure of themselves, whether they are worthy of the symbolic mandate that is bestowed upon them. As Žižek writes:

> The subject does not know why he is occupying this place in the symbolic network. His own answer to this 'Che vuoi?' of the Other can only be the hysterical question: 'Why am I what I'm supposed to be, why have I this mandate? Why am I . . . [a teacher, a master, a king . . .]?' Briefly: 'Why am I what you [the big Other] are saying that I am?' (*SO*, 113)

And this is an ambiguity, a 'dialectic' (*SO*, 112), that Žižek argues is ineradicable. It is *always* possible to ask of any symbolic statement, like Freud's famous joke about a man telling another man he is going to Cracow when he is in fact going to Cracow (*SO*, 197): what does it mean? What is it aiming at? Why is the Other telling me this? It is always possible to find another meaning behind the obvious one. It is never possible to speak literally, to occupy the Symbolic without remainder, to have the empty place and what occupies it fit perfectly. It is a mismatch that Žižek associates with a certain *enunciation* outside of any enunciated. As he writes: 'The question mark arising above the curve of "quilting" thus indicates the persistence of a gap between utterance [the enunciated] and its enunciation: at the level of utterance you are saying this, but what do you want to tell me with it, through it?' (*SO*, 111).

In other words, there is always a certain 'gap' or 'leftover' in any interpellation – but it is not a gap that can be simply got rid of, for it is just this that makes interpellation possible, that is the place from where it speaks. It is a gap that is not merely an empirical excess, something that is greater than any nomination – this is the very illusion of the master-signifier – but a kind of internal absence or void, a reminder of the fact that the message cannot be stated in advance but only after it has been identified with, is only a stand-in for that differentiality which founds the symbolic order. It is not something 'outside' or 'beyond' ideology, but that 'difference' that allows the master-signifier's naming of its own difference. (That is – and this is brought out by Žižek's successive parsing of Lacan's 'graph of desire' (*SO*, 100) in 'Che Vuoi?' – if the Symbolic makes the Imaginary possible, so this other dimension, that of the Real, makes the Symbolic possible.) As Žižek says of this relationship between ideology and what appears 'outside' of it: 'The last support of the ideological effect (of the way an ideological network of signifiers "holds" us) is the non-sensical, pre-ideological kernel of enjoyment. In ideology, "all is not ideology (that is, ideological meaning)", but it is this very surplus which is the last support of ideology' (*SO*, 124).

There is thus always a gap between interpellation and any defined symbolic meaning. Any named cause can only come up short; there is always a difference between enunciation and utterance. And yet, as we saw with the master-signifier, interpellation works best when it appears mysterious, nonsensical, incomplete, not only to us but even to the Other. For it is just this that appears to open it up to us, allow us to add to it, make it our own. It is just in its lack and unknowability that it calls upon us to realize it, take its place, say what it should be saying. However, as we saw in Chapter 1, whatever we do in response to it will always in retrospect be seen to be what it was already about. It is in its 'emptiness' that it is able to speak to all future interpretations of it, that any 'going beyond' is able to occur only in its name. It is not so much a match between a subject entirely contained within the Symbolic and a master-signifier that quilts the entire social field without remainder that we have here, but a match between a subject that feels themselves outside of the Symbolic and a master-signifier that is always different from itself. We identify not so much with any enunciated as with the position of enunciation itself. The fact that the Other does not have it, is divided from itself, is not a barrier to identification but its very condition, for just as we are completed by the Other, so this Other is completed by us. As Žižek writes: 'This lack in the Other gives the subject – so to speak – a breathing space; it enables him to avoid total alienation in the signifier not by filling out his lack but by allowing him to identify himself, his own lack, with the lack in the Other' (*SO*, 122).

This is the ambiguity of that *fantasy* with which Žižek says we fill out the gap in interpellation, just as that 'sublime object' fills out what is missing in the master-signifier. And, as with the master-signifier, the particular fantasy that Žižek takes up in order to analyse this is the anti-Semitic one. That is, in terms that almost exactly repeat what we said earlier about a certain 'in Jew more than Jew' that supplements the master-signifier of the Jew, so here with interpellation there is a kind of fantasy that behind any actual demand by Jews there is always another, that there is always something more that they want (*SO*, 114). But, again, the crucial aspect of this fantasy – as we have seen earlier with our mythical Jewish neighbour, Mr Stern – is that Jews themselves *do not have to be aware of this*. This is the meaning of Žižek's argument connecting Jews as the privileged target of such racist fantasies and the particular form of their religion. He is precisely not making the point that there is anything actually in their beliefs that would justify or explain these fantasies, but rather that the Jewish religion itself 'persists in the enigma of the Other's [that is, God's] desire' (*SO*, 115), that this Other is also a mystery to Jews themselves, that to paraphrase Hegel the mystery *of* the Jews is a mystery *to* Jews themselves. Nevertheless, it *is* this fantasy that Jews somehow *do* know what they want that operates as a supplement to interpellation. It attempts to fill out the void of the question 'Che vuoi?' with an answer. And even if we have to speak for the Other ourselves, admit the knowledge they do not recognize, this is not to break the anti-Semitic fantasy but only to render it stronger. The very incompleteness of our interpellation, the fact that things make no sense to us or that we can take a cynical distance on to the values of our society, is not at all to dispel the promise of some underlying meaning but only to make us search for one all the more.

And yet, if this distance from society and our positing of the Other are how we are interpellated, all this can also be read another way, as opening up a certain 'outside' to the system. It is not simply a matter of doing away with the ideological fantasy but of thinking what makes it possible. For if the Jew as fantasy, just as the Jew as *object a*, is able to recoup otherness and return it to the system, it also points to something else that would be required to make *this* up. That is, if the Jew as *object a* or fantasy allows the master-signifier or interpellation to be named as its own difference, it also raises the question of what allows *it* to be named. And it is *this*, finally, that Lacan means by his famous statement that 'There is no Other of the Other' (*E*, 311). It does not mean that there is *no* guarantee to the Other but that there is no *final* guarantee, that any such guarantee would always have to be underwritten in turn from somewhere else.

It means that the same element that closes off the system also opens it up, in a kind of infinite regress or psychotic foreclosure of the Name-of-the-Father. And it is at this point, as we say, that the *entire system* becomes ambiguous, that the same element that provides an answer to the 'Che vuoi?' also restates the question (*SO*, 124).[7] And what this in turn raises – in a theme we pursue throughout this book – is that, beyond thinking of the Jew as an exception that allows the universal to be constituted, we have the Jew as the 'sinthome' of a drive: the universal itself as its own exception (*ME*, 49). It is close to the ambiguity of Žižek's own work, in which the critique he proposes of the system almost repeats the system's own logic; but in repeating the system in this manner he also opens it up to something else. Again, taking us back to questions we first raised in Chapter 1 – that we can reveal the 'emptiness' at the heart of the Symbolic only by filling it in; that it is never to be seen as such but only as a retrospective effect – we would say that not only is any act or positing of the Symbolic only a repetition of it but that it is only through such a repetition that we might produce an 'act'.

Concrete universality

As we have seen, the master-signifier is always different from itself and is the name for this difference. It both reveals the void for which everything stands in and covers over this void. But in order to try to explain this in more detail, let us turn to Žižek's analysis of the difficult Hegelian concepts of 'concrete universality' and 'oppositional determination' in *For They Know Not*. 'Concrete universality' stands as the high point of the Hegelian thinking of identity – what Hegel calls 'identity-with-itself' after 'identity-in-itself' and 'identity-for-the-other' – but it is identity as the very 'impossibility of predicates, nothing but the confrontation of an entity with the void at the point where we expect a predicate, a determination of its positive content' (*TK*, 36). To take Hegel's example of 'God is God', which repeats that tautology we find in the master-signifier, in a first stage certain predicates are attributed to Him, while in a second stage He is seen as exhibiting just these attributes (but only in the form of their absence or opposite). As Hegel writes: 'Such *identical* talk therefore *contradicts* itself. Identity, instead of being in its own self truth and absolute truth, is consequently the very opposite; instead of being the unmoved simple, it is the passage beyond itself into the dissolution of itself' (*TK*, 35). And it is this that – as part of a general attack on deconstructionism – distinguishes Hegel from Derrida for Žižek. It is – again, as part of the general question of how to think 'outside' of the

master-signifier – only through the self-contradiction involved in identity that we are able to grasp its limit, and not through its simple impossibility or deferral. As Žižek writes: 'Derrida incessantly varies the motif
of how full identity-with-itself is impossible; how it is always, constitu-
tively, deferred, split . . . Yet what eludes him is the Hegelian inversion
of identity *qua* impossible into *identity itself as the name for a certain radical
impossibility*' (*TK*, 37).

But, before we develop the consequences of this, what is 'concrete universality'? How do we see it in practice? Žižek provides an example of it
in Marx's classic analysis in 'The Class Struggles in France' of how in the
1848 Revolution Republicanism emerged as the surprise outcome of the
struggle between the two competing Royalist factions, the Orléanists
and the Legitimists. As he outlines the situation there, each faction was
confronted with a problem: how best to win the battle with the other?
How to speak not merely for their own particular interpretation of the
proper royal lineage but for their opponent's as well? That is, as we
have previously seen, how not so much to refute the other empirically
as to win by proposing the very grounds of the dispute, so that no
matter what the other side argued they would ultimately be agreeing
with them? And the extraordinary thing, as Marx shows, was that each
side of the Royalist split sought to prevail by putting forward *Republicanism* as their common ground. As Žižek summarizes:

> A royalist is forced to choose between Orléanism and Legitimism –
> can he avoid the choice by choosing royalism in general, the very
> medium of the choice? Yes – by choosing to be republican, by
> placing himself at the point of intersection of the two sets of
> Orléanists and Legitimists. (*TK*, 34)

In other words, both Orléanism and Legitimism attempt to quilt the
field by claiming that they are seen even in their difference or absence.
Each argues that it is not so much either 'Orléanism' or 'Legitimism', or
even that 'Republicanism' they have in common, as the very *relationship*
between these. It is what would be different from *every* statement of itself,
even as 'Republicanism'. As Žižek goes on: ' "Republican" is thus, in
this logic, a species of the genus royalism; within the level of species, it
holds the place of the genus itself – in it, the universal genus of royalism
is represented, acquires particular existence, in the form of its opposite'
(*TK*, 34).

Or let us take another example of this 'concrete universality', this time
starting with G.K. Chesterton's famous aphorism from 'A Defence of

Detective Stories': 'Morality is the most dark and daring of conspiracies' (*TK*, 29). At first, we might understand law (morality) here simply as opposed to crime; law as what regulates crime from the outside, as though it could know what it is in advance. But, as Žižek says, paraphrasing Hegel, this would be law only in its 'abstract' identity, in which 'all actual, effective life remains out of reach' (*TK*, 33). And what this means is that, as opposed to the supposed opposition between them, the law cannot be known outside of crime; that not only (as the advance of common law attests) can we not know all crime in advance, but that the very institution of law allows crime, opens up the possibility of further crime. This would be law in its 'concrete' identity, which includes crime as a 'sublated moment of the wealth of its content' (*TK*, 33). And this would be a little as we saw with the second stage in the constitution of the master-signifier, in which the law is never to be grasped as such but only as crime, as what all various crimes have in common. Law is never to be seen as such but only as its exception; and yet this *is* what the law is. Law *is* the name for its own exception, its difference from itself. However, we have still not got to the final 'concrete universal' – like that third stage of the master-signifier – until we understand that *no* statement of the law, even as its own exception, even as what all crimes have in common, can ever take anything but the form of *another* crime or exception. Law is not merely the difference between crimes, but is always different *from itself*. The very relationship between law and crime – the ability of law to be the genus of the species crime – can only take the form of a crime, an exception. The universal (law) itself is only another crime. As Žižek writes:

> Law 'dominates' crime when some 'absolute crime' particularizes all other crimes, converts them into mere particular crimes – and this gesture of universalization by means of which an entity turns into its opposite is, of course, precisely that of *point de capiton*. (*TK*, 33)

To put this another way, 'concrete universality' is that 'uncanny point at which the universal genus encounters itself within its own particular species' (*TK*, 34) – and encounters itself in the form of its opposite. And two conclusions can be drawn from this dialectical 'coincidence' of genus and species. First, any attempt to speak of this genus only turns it into another species; and, second, this occurs because of the opposite of this genus, or that of which this genus is the opposite, the very difference between genus and species, which both stand in for. And the final 'identity-with-itself' of this universal genus is that it *is* the void of its inscription in this sense. The universal just *is* this problem of being able to relate to itself only in the form of the particular. It *is* only its impossibility, the fact that any statement of it can only be particular. The universal is at once what ensures that there are only particulars and what means that the particular is never merely particular, but always stands in for something else, is the failure to be universal (*CHU*, 216–17). However, what this implies is that there is a kind of infinite regress at stake in concrete universality, in a continual 'doubling of the universal when it is confronted with its particular content' (*TK*, 34). *Any* statement of the universal is only to stand in for that void that would allow it, is only the real universal's absence or opposite. And, again, this infinite regress, this failure of identity, would be what the master-signifier is; but this itself cannot be stated without a certain 'remainder'; there is always left out that difference or 'empty place' (*TK*, 44) that allows this to be said. We never actually have that final 'reconciliation' between figure and ground or species and genus, for there is always something excluded – the place of enunciation – that enables this.

This is the complexity – to return to those issues we raised at the beginning of this chapter – of Žižek's attempt to think antagonism (*object a*) outside of the master-signifier. As we have already seen, in the early part of his career, at the time of *Sublime Object*, Žižek follows Laclau and Mouffe's project of 'radical democracy': the elevation of one particular term from the ideological field and making it the master-signifier of the rest. But the decisive 'anti-essentialist' gesture – this is how it differs from Marx's and Althusser's concept of overdetermination – is that it is not one element given in advance that quilts the others, but that any one of them might be it (*SO*, 4). And yet, as Žižek's work goes on – and this is perhaps made most explicit in his dialogue with Laclau in *Contingency, Hegemony, Universality* – he begins to take a distance from this 'radical democracy' for not properly taking into account what he calls 'external difference' (*CHU*, 92), which is not that difference between competing signifiers within the existing symbolic horizon but what is excluded to allow this horizon. That is, Žižek wants to think not how one master-signifier speaks for others, but what allows the master-signifier as such. He wants to think not the master-signifier as that void for which others stand in, but that void for which the master-signifier itself stands in (*CHU*, 108). And it is at this point that Žižek unexpectedly turns to the once-rejected notion of 'class' as the best way of thinking this difference outside of the Symbolic, this void which allows the master-signifier. As he writes, citing Marx against Laclau's argument against 'class' as the ultimate master-signifier:

One should counter [Laclau's objections] by the already-mentioned paradox of 'oppositional determination', of the *part* of the chain that sustains its *horizon* itself: class antagonism certainly appears as one in the series of social antagonisms, but it is simultaneously the specific antagonism which 'predominates over the rest, whose relations thus assign rank and influence to the others'. (*CHU*, 320)

But, in this context, what exactly does Žižek mean by 'class'? What is at stake in conceiving the constitution of the social not in terms of 'radical democracy' but 'class'? As we suggest, it is for Žižek a way of thinking not so much the universality allowed by the master-signifier as what allows this universality. It is a way of thinking the underlying 'antagonism' of society, which is not some empirical excess outside of the social but a kind of impossibility within it. In other words, what Žižek fundamentally accuses Laclau of is that he does not think the third and final stage of the master-signifier: that 'concrete universality' in which a thing includes itself, is not merely that difference that allows the identity or equivalence of others but is always different from itself (*CHU*, 130–31). Class is, in that contest of hegemonization that Laclau speaks of, that which explains the values of 'radical democracy' and all those other signifiers and quilts them together. But it is also an attempt to speak of the void that allows any master-signifier, that any master-signifier only stands in for. And it is just this, again, that 'radical democracy' does not do in operating only within the horizon of an already existing universality. It is unable to imagine a truly radical social 'act', the realization or incorporation of this 'antagonism' in making the universal and particular the same, but only an endless series of substitutions *within* this universality. As Žižek will say in his collection *Revolution at the Gates*, in pointing out the status of 'class' as the impossible 'coincidence' of species and genus, particular and universal, internal and external difference:

> For Marx, of course, the only universal class whose singularity (exclusion from the society of property) guarantees its actual universality is the proletariat. This is what Ernesto Laclau rejects in his version of hegemony: for Laclau, the short circuit between the Universal and the Particular is *always* illusory, temporary, a kind of 'transcendental paralogism'. (*L*, 297)

But to make the ambiguity of Žižek's gesture of thinking 'class' clearer, he will go on to speak of it as a 'symptom' in *Revolution at the Gates* (*L*, 254–6, 267–8, 332). It is a symptom that, as we have seen when we looked at the Jew, is the sign for a certain impossibility of society. It is what allows us to think an 'outside' to the social, what has to be excluded from it in order for it to be constituted. And yet we can see the 'virtuality' of this symptom, the difficulty of speaking in its name, in another example of it that Žižek discusses in *Sublime Object*: the notion of 'freedom', as analysed by Marx (*SO*, 21–3). In bourgeois society, we have a number of freedoms, including the freedom to sell our labour – but this last is a freedom that leads to the enslavement of the worker and the negation of all those other freedoms. Here, as Žižek puts it, in a 'concrete' as distinct from an 'abstract' freedom, the genus of (bourgeois) freedom meets its opposite in the form of one of its species: the freedom to sell our labour. And it is now this freedom that becomes the true universal, of which bourgeois freedom is only a particular. That is, the various bourgeois freedoms (the freedom of speech, of assembly, of commerce) are only guaranteed within capitalism by this other freedom: the freedom to sell our labour. It is this 'freedom' that makes all the others possible, for which they all stand in. But, of course, this leads to the problem that we cannot really say that this freedom to sell our labour is a distortion of some 'true' quality of freedom, because this freedom is only possible because of it. And this is to say that antagonism is not really outside of the master-signifier because it can only be expressed in terms of it. If it can only be experienced in a 'distorted' way – as with 'freedom' here – this is not because we actually see it as distorted, but because we see it *as a master-signifier*. Antagonism is not so much the failure of the master-signifier as it is the master-signifier itself. Just as the master-signifier is seen in its very absence or impossibility, so this antagonism exists as what it is not: the master-signifier. Antagonism is not some opposition or alternative to what is; but what is arises only in response to antagonism.[8] As Žižek says, antagonism as the true difference, as what is more universal than any universal, is only those 'particular differences internal to the system' (*CHU*, 92).

So, to return to class: what really is at stake in thinking of antagonism in terms of class? We might begin here with Žižek's description of class as the 'properly temporal-dialectical tension between the universal and the particular' (*L*, 298) (terms which are, incidentally, almost exactly the same as those he uses to describe the Jew in *Metastases*). In one sense, then, it is impossible to bring the universal and the particular together: as Laclau says, any attempted equivalence between them is always illusory. And Žižek in his early work agrees with this: it is what he means by the 'king as the place-holder of the void' (*TK*, 267) revealing the locus of power to be empty. But, in another sense, we must keep on trying to

make the universal and the particular the same. It is only through this
attempted making-equivalent that we can reveal the true universal,
which is not some empty frame that the particular seeks to fill (as it is
for Laclau), but only that place from where this equivalence is stated.
(And this is what Žižek can already be understood to mean by the 'king
as the place-holder of the void': that it is only through the king's filling-
out of this empty place that we are able to see that void which allows it.)
It is a question no longer of an *exception* (what cannot be spoken of or
filled in) that allows a *universal*, but of a '*sinthome*' connected to a *drive*
(in which any universal is always revealed as an exception). And it is
this that Žižek means by class: not a master-signifier that is proved by
its exception (by its own absence or impossibility), but – only the slight-
est twist – this constant process of self-exception itself, in which at once
there is no exception to this process and we cannot exactly say what this
process is because it is its own exception.

This is why, to conclude, if Žižek speaks of 'class', he insists that it is
not to be thought of in the old scientific, objectivist way. He agrees with
Laclau on this, and even goes further than him (*CHU*, 319–20). That is,
if he speaks of class, it is not finally to go back to the notion of overdetermination, or even to say what is excluded from society, as though this
could be named. Rather, it is to argue that the social is complete only
because of class (struggle), takes the place of class (struggle). The social
is explained by class, just as with any master-signifier; but class is not
some exception that would render it whole, precisely because it does
not stand outside of it. Instead, class renders the social 'not-all' (*TK*,
44): there is at once no exception to the social and the social (as represented by the proletariat) is its own exception. To put this another way,
one of Hegel's arguments – this *is* his concept of 'concrete universality' – is that, if a certain notion does not add up to itself, this lack is
reflected back into the notion and the notion itself changes (*CHU*, 99–
100). And we could say the same about class: unlike 'radical democracy', which ultimately wants to take its own failure into account from
somewhere outside of it, with the 'failure' of class the notion itself
changes. Class – as universal – is nothing but its own failure. And this
is what Hegel means by the *Absolute Spirit*: not the panlogist sublation of
every difference but simply the 'succession of all dialectical transforma-
tions, the impossibility of establishing a final overlapping between the
universal and the particular' (*CHU*, 60). And this is indicated by the
fact that in *Contingency, Hegemony, Universality* Žižek has several names
for this 'class' as universal: sexual difference, the Real, even capital
itself. And perhaps even 'behind' all of these, as another word for it, is

the *subject* (just as the proletariat is the universal 'subject' of history). It is subject in that sense we spoke of in Chapter 1 as the only true topic of philosophy. Class as split between the master-signifier and *object a* is exactly like that 'split subject' we looked at there. This is the final ambiguity of the master-signifier: it is its own opposite (*object a*); but it is an opposite – this is perhaps what Žižek does not pay enough attention to in 'Why is Every Act?' – that leads only to another master-signifier, that can be seen only through another master-signifier. And in our next chapter, we turn to the 'other' side of this in trying to think this *object a* as that 'act' that allows or results from the master-signifier.

Chapter 3

What is an act?

What is an act? Žižek provides many examples of it throughout his work. It can be seen in such personal moments as Kevin Kline blurting out 'I'm gay' instead of 'Yes!' during his wedding ceremony in *In and Out* (*CHU*, 122). It can be seen in Mel Gibson not conceding to his son's kidnappers' demands but vowing to come after them no matter what the consequences in the film *Ransom* (*CHU*, 122). It can be seen in criminal mastermind Keyser Soeze, upon finding his wife and daughter held hostage by a rival gang, shooting them so that they no longer have any hold over him in the film *The Usual Suspects* (*CHU*, 122). It can be seen in such events occurring within the existing political structure as President Clinton's attempts to reform American Medicare, against both the attacks on the public sector and the interests of the big drug companies (*B*, 115). It can be seen in the abolition of the death penalty in Mitterrand's France and the passing of divorce laws in staunchly Catholic Italy (*TS*, 134). It can be seen in Lacan's dissolution of the Ecole freudienne de Paris, the basis of his institutional power and prestige, just before his death in 1979 (*CHU*, 123). It can be seen, finally, in such world-historical events that overturn whole social and political structures and bring about new systems of belief as the death and resurrection of Christ and the spread of the Catholic Church under St Paul (*TS*, 141), the overthrow of the monarchy and the birth of democracy in the French Revolution of 1789 (*TS*, 136, 196), the abolition of tsarism and the establishment of communism in the Russian Revolution of 1917 (*T?*, 114–17; *L*, 5), and perhaps even the flying of planes into the World Trade Center and the opening up of some alternative to the hegemony of the West on 11 September 2001 (*DR*, 49, 154).

What is involved in these acts? What do they have in common? In one way, they all break with the existing symbolic conventions. They do not remain within the range of commonly accepted possibilities, but actively seek to expand them. There is always an element of the unexpected and unpredictable associated with the act, of something not foreseeable within the current conceptual horizons. And this means that if the act necessarily arises from within the old symbolic order it cannot entirely be named or judged within this order. Its very aim is to redefine what is possible, to change the criteria by which it will be understood. To this extent, the act, in so far as it is successful, can only be spoken of in its own terms. It transforms the symbolic context, so that, after it, it does indeed seem possible. Thus, after the abolition of capital punishment in France or the passage of divorce laws in Italy, it can be said that the people were already willing to accept such a change. After the French or Russian Revolutions, it can be argued that the objective conditions for such upheavals already existed. But what must be kept in mind is that all this comes about only *because* of the act. It is the act itself that makes what takes place appear achievable, no more than the actualization of an already existing possibility. As Žižek writes:

> An act does not occur *within* the given horizon of what appears to be 'possible' – it redefines the very contours of what is possible (an act accomplishes what, within the given symbolic universe, appears to be 'impossible', yet it changes its conditions so that it creates retroactively the conditions of its own possibility). (*CHU*, 121)

What, then, to return to that question we left unanswered at the end of the last chapter, is the relationship of the act to the master-signifier? In so far as the act breaks with the symbolic order, is it to be opposed to it? In so far as the act reshapes the symbolic order, is it to be identified with it? Is the act the passage between two different symbolic orders or between two different states of the same symbolic order? Or is it, on the contrary, what founds the symbolic order, but what must be covered over or effaced by it? To begin with, the act is not simply to be *opposed* to the symbolic order. As Žižek writes in *Indivisible Remainder*, that book of his, along with *Ticklish Subject*, where he most extensively considers the act: 'The Act and the Big Other [the symbolic order], far from being opposed, are intertwined in a constitutive way' (*IR*, 143). But does this therefore mean that they are the *same*? This is where the complicated questions arise. Later in *Indivisible Remainder*, Žižek will suggest that, even though from the point of view of the master-signifier the two cannot be separated, there is nevertheless a distinction we might draw between them. The act and the master-signifier are the two sides of 'one and the same entity'; but the act is to grasp it in the mode of 'becoming' and the master-signifier in the mode of 'being' (*IR*, 147).

But the terms of this distinction must be understood very carefully. It is not, despite what Žižek might appear to be saying, simply
a matter of conceiving of the act as a potential master-signifier, as a
master-signifier about-to-be. And this for two reasons. The first is that,
in so far as this is so, what is to stop us from imagining – as others have
done when they speak of the 'end of history' – that, even if not now, at
some time in the future, all further acts will be realized, that there will be
no more acts to come? That is, in so far as the act is understood as merely
a potential master-signifier, why would it not realize itself without
remainder? Or, to put this another way, if there are ultimately only
master-signifiers and master-signifiers about-to-be, why is the act necessary in the first place? Why do we need the act at all? The second reason
is that to the extent that we continue to understand the act as always
only potential or in-between, we cannot but think that to speak about it
is to betray it, reduce it, miss something about it. We could only ever say
what it is in retrospect, after it has become a master-signifier; but we
thereby lose the sense of risk, of undecidability, of everything not being
determined in advance, that we feel characterizes the act. (Perhaps
it is even the act itself that sutures up the gap like this, that makes it seem
as though things were always the way they are now.) And, finally, what
must be understood is that these two attitudes towards the act go
together: that we could think of the Symbolic doing away with the act
only for it to be necessary to explain it because of some impossible act
outside of it; that we could think of the act as a certain potential always
outside of the Symbolic only for it to end up being exhausted within it.

So what, again, is an act? How are we to think what Žižek might mean
by speaking of it as a 'becoming' as opposed to a 'being' without resort-
ing to the classic philosophical opposition between the potential and the
actual, without making the act merely a master-signifier about-to-be or
only possible from the beginning because of the master-signifier? In fact,
in order to reclaim the radical sense of act that Žižek intends, we would
say that it is necessary to *invert* that common-sense understanding of it
that we have just outlined. We would argue that it is not so much a
matter of an act standing outside of the master-signifier as potential to
actual as of what already in the master-signifier renders its actuality
only potential. The act does not so much come before the master-
signifier as a master-signifier about-to-be as 'after' the master-signifier
to reveal it as the act it once was. That is, it is not a matter of an undecidability (potential) becoming decidable (actual), but of an undecidability being opened up in what was previously decided. It is, as it were, only
after the master-signifier that we can see those alternatives excluded by

it – and this is the act (*TS*, 138). To think this act – and this is why it is not so much opposed to the master-signifier as the master-signifier seen another way – is to think what is left out of the master-signifier, a kind of potentiality (or, better, virtuality) that *doubles* the master-signifier. To think the act, therefore, is to think not so much something before the master-signifier (for, as we have seen, there is nothing before or outside of the master-signifier) as something *at the same time as* the master-signifier. At the same time as the master-signifier, as the fact that everything can only be seen through the master-signifier, what is revealed is that this is only possible because of the act.

The act, then, is a certain *doubling* of the master-signifier. In that way we began to touch on towards the end of the previous chapter with regard to the 'antagonism' of class – which does not just occur within the symbolic order but also opens up that void for which the symbolic order stands in – the act both is what each master-signifier responds to and can only take the form of another master-signifier. It is a limit to the master-signifier, but a limit that can only be seen within the master-signifier. It is a limit to the master-signifier, but a limit that makes the master-signifier total. In this, to use a language Žižek will have more and more resort to, the act makes the master-signifier at once necessary and impossible. The extension of the master-signifier will go on forever, covering all fields – as Žižek will document in *Plague of Fantasies* – but all of this only because of an always excluded 'act'. And this is to say that, as opposed to the act as some potential that is actualized or some undecidability that is resolved, the act at once has already taken place (for the master-signifier to exist at all) and will never take place (for it can be seen only in terms of the master-signifier). And, in another way, it is always taking place, for it occurs precisely *at the same time as* the master-signifier. The act, to use words from Lacan's Twentieth Seminar, is that which 'doesn't stop (not) being written' (*S20*, 59) – or, in Žižek's words, taken from Schelling, is 'Absolute' or 'Eternal' (*IR*, 21). It is this difficult insight that Žižek pursues in his work – an insight that we try to follow here. It is an insight that we even hold against Žižek, who at times can indeed be seen to speak of the act in terms of a potential becoming actual, a 'becoming' turning into 'being'. But this criticism is not our main concern here (we will take it up in more detail in Chapter 5). Rather, it is to try to develop the consequences of this novel conception of the act (although we will see it going back at least to Schelling), and how it connects with other aspects of Žižek's work: the question of enunciation we looked at in Chapter 1; the antagonism and perpetual requilting of Chapter 2; the feminine 'not-all' and the drive of Chapter 4. It is a difficult insight not only because it breaks with the common-sense notion of the act or decision as the resolution of an otherwise ambiguous or undecidable situation but because it implies that the decision itself actually reveals or produces a certain undecidability. But what is the nature of this undecidability? What would it mean to say that the act of decision and this undecidability are inseparable? And what would be the ultimate status of this undecidability, if it is only ever virtual, not so much an alternative to things as they are as what is excluded by every alternative?

It is these questions that we seek to answer here through a reading of three of Žižek's texts, which are taken up in chronological order: his commentary on Walter Benjamin's famous 'Theses on the Philosophy of History' in the chapter 'You Only Die Twice' of *Sublime Object*; his analysis of Schelling's various *Weltalter* drafts in the first two chapters of *Indivisible Remainder*; and his engagement with the work of the contemporary French political philosopher Alain Badiou in the chapter 'The Politics of Truth' of *Ticklish Subject*. Beneath all of these, we come back to the fundamental question posed by this book: what is the relationship between the master-signifier and *object a* in Žižek's work? To what extent does Žižek think that *object a* precedes the master-signifier? To what extent is it seen as an *external* limit to the master-signifier, as what it eventually sublimates or overcomes? To what extent is it seen as an *internal* limit to the master-signifier, something the master-signifier can never finally overcome because it *is* the master-signifier? And, as we have tried to argue here, these are precisely the same questions as those raised by the act in its relationship to the master-signifier. Take, for example, the following passage from *Ticklish Subject*, in which Žižek paraphrases against Badiou the 'Lacanian' position on the relationship of 'negativity' (we might say the act) to 'enthusiastic identification' (we might say the master-signifier):

> For Lacan, negativity, a negative gesture of withdrawal, precedes any positive gesture of enthusiastic identification with a Cause: negativity functions as the condition of (im)possibility of the enthusiastic identification – that is to say, it lays the ground, opens up space for it, but is simultaneously obfuscated by it and undermines it. (*TS*, 154)

Here we have the idea that this 'negativity' – the negativity of the act – is an internal limit to the master-signifier; but we still perhaps have the sense that it is simply the *transcendental* condition of the master-signifier, as though it comes before it and can be seen outside of it. We still do not have the *simultaneity* of the act and the master-signifier, the realization that while the act makes the master-signifier possible it is only able to be seen through it. It is undoubtedy an impossible simultaneity to think – it is the true Real in Žižek's work – but it is nonetheless this simultaneity that is at stake here and against which we seek to judge Žižek.

'Theses on the Philosophy of History'

How to think this act? How to avoid conceiving of it as the passage from the potential to the actual? How to resist the temptation to understand it either as the product of the will or as doing away with the will? How to grasp it as a repetition, but a repetition that would not exist without the act? In order to answer these questions, let us turn to a text that Žižek often takes up in his work: Walter Benjamin's 'Theses on the Philosophy of History'. This late essay by Benjamin is undoubtedly best known for its statement that history is written by the 'victors' and for revealing the surprising influence of theology on Benjamin's Marxism. As Benjamin writes, using the extraordinary analogy of a midget hidden inside a chess machine:

> The story is told of an automaton constructed in such a way that it could play a winning game of chess, answering each move of an opponent with a countermove . . . One can imagine a philosophical counterpart to this device. The puppet called 'dialectical materialism' is to win all the time. It can easily be a match for anyone if it enlists the service of theology, which today, as we know, is wizened and has to keep out of sight. (*SO*, 136)

That is, for Benjamin, if the scientific laws of dialectical materialism are always to win, to provide an explanation for everything, they nevertheless rely upon a secret theological force, a *deus ex machina*, an *act*. But, importantly, this act is not to be understood in any positivist or substantialist sense. As Benjamin makes clear, this human player must always remain hidden, can never be seen as themselves, but can operate only through the guise of a machine. They are the kind of 'subject' we always assume when we play chess against a computer: transferential, doubling, ghost-like.

How do we see this 'subject' in Benjamin's text? 'Theses on the Philosophy of History' is characterized by its rejection of perhaps the two dominant schools of historical interpretation. On the one hand, it rejects the so-called 'hermeneutical' notion that in order to know the past it is necessary to suspend our knowledge of the present and grasp historical events in their own terms, as they actually occurred. It rejects the idea of ' "accustoming ourselves to the past" by abstracting our actual historical position, the place from where we are speaking' (*SO*, 133). And, on the other hand, it rejects the notion that we can see the past only through the present, that the past is merely a series of competing interpretations with no way of choosing between them. It rejects any kind of ' "will to power as interpretation", as the right of the winner to "write his own history", to impose his own "perspective" ' (*SO*, 138). For Benjamin, these two approaches, although they might appear to be opposed, are in fact the same. Both rely upon the notion that we can somehow take the present into account: in the first, that we can bracket it off; in the second, that we can speak of it, know that it is where we stand. As opposed to this *historicism*, in which in one way or another the past is relativized by the present (in the first approach, it is only from the point of view of the present that we can speak the truth of the past; in the second, it is only from the point of view of the present that we can speak the lack of truth of the past), Benjamin insists that in the proper conception of history it is not the past but the *present* that is relativized.[1] As Žižek writes:

> What we are claiming [of Benjamin] is something much more radical: what the proper *historical* stance (as opposed to historicism) 'relativizes' is not the past (always distorted by our present point of view) but, paradoxically, *the present itself* – our present can be conceived only as the outcome (not only of what happened in the past, but also) of the crushed potentials for the future that were contained in the past. (*FA*, 90)

But what does Benjamin hold up against this 'continuum' (*SO*, 140), in which the present flows from the past and the past can only be seen in terms of the present? How to think a history that is not that of the victors, or that does not simply substitute one set of victors for another? For Benjamin, as opposed to both of those approaches above, the true aim of historical interpretation is to 'appropriate the past in itself in so far as it is "open", in so far as the "yearning for redemption" is already at work in it' (*SO*, 138). But what could he mean by this odd oxymoron? How could it be a matter of knowing the past 'in itself', but only in so far as it is 'open'? On the one hand, Benjamin is not opposed to the promise of hermeneutism: we *can* know the past in itself. But, on the other hand, as opposed to the practice of hermeneutism, we can know the past in itself not by overcoming the prejudices and preconceptions of the present but only because the past is an effect of the present. However, precisely because the past *is* only an effect of the present, this is to say that any such present is itself inevitably subject to another future rewriting, which is able to show how it too is part of the past, determined by it in a way it cannot see. That is, just as the past, so the present is perpetually available to future rewriting. Just as each present is able to bring out different qualities in the past, show that it is always undetermined, so the future is able to do this to the present. We are always able to make a connection between the present and the past, show that any present is only a continuation of the past; but only in so far as it is subject to the same rewriting as it, in so far as it is 'open' like it. It is not a matter of the present seeing the past in its image, making it over from some point outside of it; but the present *is* the past, the present can know the past 'in itself', only in so far as *both* are 'open', able to be rewritten from some point in the future. And *this* is the profound insight of Benjamin's method: as opposed to historicism, which speaks of our place in history but only from somewhere outside of it, it is only this 'messianic' (*SO*, 139), open-ended future, which is absolutely outside of history, that ensures that we are always in history, that there is nothing outside of history, that the present is a direct continuation of the past 'in itself'.[2]

But, again, what is meant by this? When Benjamin speaks of a certain 'yearning for redemption' at stake in history, his aim is to think what is excluded from it, what is left out by it. From the vantage point of the present, he seeks to bring out the repressed revolutionary potential, the 'missed revolutionary chance' (*SO*, 139), of the past. But why is this not merely the privilege of rewriting history granted to the victors? Why is this not a so-called 'revolutionary potential' granted to anyone who wants to see it? Indeed, this possibility of knowing the past in itself *is* the idea that the past does not exist outside of the present, that there is nothing else of the past but our present perspective on to it. Each successive present *does* construct the past in its image, does bring about the history that retrospectively justifies it. Benjamin here is not simply opposed to historicism and the idea that history is written by the victors. But, as we suggest, what this necessarily implies is the possibility of *another* always being able to come along afterwards and seeing a connection between the past and the present that the present cannot see. And *this* is what Benjamin means by redeeming the repressed 'revolutionary potential' of history. It is not so much some actual alternative that is to be brought about, because whatever it is it will always be seen as no more than what was already implicit in the past, as what is excluded to ensure that this is always so. 'Revolutionary potential' is not so much something to be actualized by being put into history as what allows us to realize what is lost by putting *anything* into history. It is at once what allows us to think this lost potential from some 'messianic' point in the future and it is what means that this potential is always lost in so far as it *is* put into history, in so far as it can be shown to be a continuation of the past. This is the paradox Žižek notes of Benjamin's position, in which the revolution is nothing more than the realization of the very *failure* of the revolution: 'The actual revolutionary conjunction functions as a condensation of past missed revolutionary chances repeating themselves in the actual revolution' (*SO*, 139).

In all of this – and, again, this is to show that it is not a matter of any opposition between Benjamin's 'messianism' and historicism – Žižek is quite right to emphasize the anti-evolutionary, anti-teleological implications of Benjamin's argument. But what Žižek has to say on this must be read very carefully. He compares Benjamin's method to Marx's famous statement that, with regard to the analysis of capitalism, we should not understand the human by the ape but the ape by the human (*FA*, 91). This is the idea that it is not possible historically to describe the advent of capitalism because – no matter how hard we try not to – we already assume that capitalism is in place. We can only see all previous social formations as imperfect versions of capitalism, as leading up to capitalism. As Žižek says, the trouble with these historical accounts is that they necessarily imagine the past as complete, with no other destiny than what came to pass. But when Benjamin rejects this in arguing that history is 'open', that things could have turned out 'otherwise', it is not simply a matter of *reversing* this and reading time backwards, for it is just this idea of the future explaining the past that he is opposing. Anti-evolutionism is merely evolutionism seen another way. Rather, what Benjamin – and, indeed, Marx – must be understood as trying to do through this reversal is to suggest the fundamentally circular nature of *all* historical analysis. And that what he is seeking to do in thinking this circularity is to recover what is excluded by this circularity, by *any* realization of the past from the point of view of the present. And what is this? Again, as a kind of summary of all we have said so far, it is not anything actual, which could only be written back into history, but precisely that future moment which allows us to realize that the present is merely a continuation of the past, that freedom involved in creating this circularity. And it is *this* that introduces a split into history, reveals a possibility that has not been seen before: this 'act' that allows the 'continuum' of history to be constructed, by means of which the present can always be seen to be connected (seemingly without the necessity of any act) to the past. We might illustrate this with a diagram taken from Žižek's *Enjoy Your Symptom!* (*E!*, 48):

How to understand this 'act' that at once appears and disappears? How to grasp this circularity – which explains everything – that is only possible from a point outside of it? We might begin here by noting an odd coincidence in Žižek's text. In the course of his discussion of Benjamin's 'Theses', Žižek quotes a passage from Lacan's First Seminar, in which he speaks of the cybernetician Norbert Weiner's notion of an 'inverted temporal dimension', but without really saying much more (*SO*, 141). Intriguingly, some hundred pages earlier in *Sublime Object*, Žižek quotes from the same passage of the Seminar, noting that to his knowledge it is the only time in his oeuvre that Lacan mentions the idea of time-travel. Now, putting these two references together, the question might be asked: how does Benjamin's concept of history imply the possibility of time-travel? Or, more specifically, how is the relationship of Benjamin's 'messianic' history to history like the relationship of time-travel to time? Let us take what is perhaps the most basic form of the time-travel scenario found in science-fiction stories, the so-called time-loop or time-paradox. It is a story in which the time-traveller journeys into the future, writes down the plans for a time-travel machine, and then sends them back to themselves in the past so that they can then build one to travel into the future. What is the real enigma here? It is not simply that the scientist or researcher is able to travel into either the future or past. After all, this is what is 'explained' by the existence of the time-machine. Rather, it is the possibility that the time-traveller, by the very act of deciding to travel into the past, subtly alters the complex chain of causes and effects that led to them doing so in the first place. As a result, nothing in the past ends up being able to explain the decision – we can never exactly repeat events the same way – and yet this only because the decision has already been made. And in a good time-travel narrative, this 'indecision' takes place at every moment. *Every* moment on the time-traveller's circuit absolutely must have happened the way it did for it to be completed *and* is entirely open, a moment when events might have turned out differently. Indeed, it is only because the decision has been made, because events do repeat themselves, because the circle is complete, that we are able to think that the decision might not have been made, that everything might have turned out differently, that the circle might have been broken. The decision is at once necessary (everything has already happened) and impossible (always deferred), one because of the other.

All this is what is at stake in that 'arrest' (*SO*, 139) of historical time we see in Benjamin's 'messianism'. This 'arrest', this act of grasping the hidden revolutionary potential in a situation in a kind of stopping of time, holds, to put it in terms of language (*SO*, 141), the place of a certain excluded diachronic element that allows the formation of a synchronic system (and, as with Žižek's discussion of this in *For They Know Not*, this fantasy of time-travel is fundamentally a fantasy of the primal scene, of seeing our own conception). That is, what we have in historicism, as in language, is a synchronic system, in which every part is dependent for its meaning on every other part: the past and the future are intertwined. This is the difficulty of thinking anything as the origin of such a system (for example, of capitalism), for as soon as we say what it is, we find that it is preceded by another, that it can only be understood in terms of the system itself. But precisely what Benjamin is trying to imagine is what is excluded to allow *this*. What does *any* historical explanation, which is ultimately only the fantasy of witnessing our own origins, stand in for? Is there not a kind of primal 'act' or 'trauma' that every named act takes the place of, which allows this 'fantasy' of entirely accounting for ourselves, of seeing ourselves from somewhere else? As Žižek writes (and, again, there is raised here the question of that 'split subject' we have spoken of before):

> The very emergence of a synchronous symbolic order implies a gap, a discontinuity in the diachronic causal chain that led up to it, a 'missing link' in the chain. Fantasy [the fantasy, we might say, of time-travel or indeed of historical explanation] is an *a contrario* proof that the status of the subject is that of a 'missing link', of a void which, within the synchronous set, holds the place of its foreclosed diachronic genesis. (*TK*, 198)

It is in this sense that Žižek speaks of what he calls, after Fredric Jameson, the 'vanishing mediator'. In its initial meaning, the vanishing mediator refers to those otherwise invisible or overlooked moments in major historical processes. It is an attempt to historicize those shifts, to provide some intermediary or mediating cause for them. The comparison might be made to something like the 'butterfly effect' in chaos physics, in which a small, almost indiscernible action leads to a vast and seemingly unrelated reaction. Examples of this 'vanishing mediator' that Žižek cites in his work include: the role of Protestantism in the rise of capitalism (*TK*, 182; *MI*, 14); the part of opposition socialist parties in the fall of communism (*TK*, 187; *TN*, 230; *E!*, 90); and perhaps even the place of Lenin in the final triumph of Stalinism (*L*, 193). But we also see this 'vanishing mediator' in such small-scale events as the first defiance of a policeman's orders in the Shah's Iran (*TN*, 233) or a crowd's disbelief in Ceauşescu's Romania (*TN*, 234). However, Žižek does not follow this usual understanding of the 'vanishing mediator', and in some ways even argues against it. For him, the 'vanishing mediator' is not to be used to historicize an event, to provide a more detailed causal explanation of it, but – to paraphrase Benjamin – is a kind of 'arrest' or stopping-point that stands in for the excluded diachronic dimension of *any* historical explanation. That is, like the act itself, the vanishing mediator is not simply to be written back into the historical record, because it is also what must be left out for this record to be constituted. And if it testifies to a certain moment of 'undecidability' in the unfolding of events, a moment when things hung in the balance and could have turned out differently, it is an 'undecidability' that is only thinkable against the background of how events actually did turn out, an 'undecidabilty' that is not to be realized but that haunts and makes possible every reality. It is an 'undecidability' – like Benjamin's 'revolutionary potential', like *object a* – that comes about only as its loss, that exists in the very form of its loss.[3] To put this another way, that moment of Protestantism is not important until capitalism supplants it; the socialist opposition parties are not significant until communism is overthrown; and perhaps even Lenin's true meaning is to be found only in Stalinism.

To return, finally, to the analogy of time-travel: is this not what we see there too? Žižek, in *Sublime Object*, speaks of a time-travel story in which a group of scientists attempt to move a cube back and forth in time ('Experiment', by Fredric Brown). There is a moment in the plot when one of them changes their mind half-way through the process, thus altering the past – and, as we tried to make clear, these changes of mind, our inability to repeat our original decision, are the real problem of time-travel, when as it were the very chain of events unleashed by our decision to travel back in time leads to that same decision not being made. And this is analogous to the way that in the true act – as we have already seen in 'Why is Every Act?' – the subject is split or does not remain the same. Brown writes of the consequences of this sudden decision not to send the

cube back into the past, thus irrevocably altering those events that led
to the present:

> 'An interesting idea,' Professor Johnson said. 'I had not thought of
> it, and it will be interesting to try. Very well, I shall *not* . . .'
> There was no paradox at all. The cube remained.
> But the rest of the universe, professors and all, vanished. (*SO*, 162)

The vanishing mediator is like this cube. For the truth is that, far from
vanishing, it is the one thing, in all of its different guises, that always
remains the same. It is what we eventually stumble over in any attempt
to explain something historically, what resists when all else has been
rationalized. To put it another way, in the time-travel story, everything is accounted for: the future explains the past as the past leads to the
future. And yet there is one thing that cannot be accounted for − and
that is the decision to travel back into time in the first place. And,
again, if this decision is no sooner named than it is shown to be overde-
termined, explained by a whole series of causes and effects, in another
way this system is not possible until *after* this decision; this system is nothing but the infinite attempt to take the place of, explain, this decision.
If this decision is infinitely predicted, must already have occurred for a
symbolic order to exist at all, it is also impossible to explain; it comes
about only through an extraordinary act of will. For the true enigma of
time-travel scenarios − from the *Terminator* series through to *Groundhog
Day* − is why, if the future has already been determined, if future events
must already have happened for the present to be the way it is, do we
nevertheless have the sense that events could go astray at any moment,
that things could turn out otherwise? At once − as revealed in Zeno's
paradoxes (*LA*, 3−6) and Benjamin's 'messianic' history − there is no
difference between any two moments (the future is already in the past)
and we can never get from one moment to the next (an infinite distance
lies between them). At each moment − this again is the meaning behind
Benjamin's paradoxical insistence that we can know the past 'in itself'
only in so far as it is 'open' − the circle is closed, the decision has already
been made, no act is necessary, and the future is uncertain, no decision
has been made, only an act of supreme will can get us from one moment
to the next. The circle is what does away with the will, what means that
there is no need for a decision; and the circle is possible only because of a
decision, is the one thing that demands that there must be a decision.
And we see in all of this − to return to 'Why is Every Act?' − that repetition and the act are not opposed, but that each implies the other, each is
possible only because of the other.

Schelling

Žižek returns to this thinking of the act in *Indivisible Remainder*. The question he seeks to resolve there, following *Sublime Object*, is: what is the status of this other possibility that the act renders visible? How is it at once revealed and covered over by the act? Žižek addresses this in *Indivisible Remainder* by looking at the work of the philosopher Schelling, and particularly at his series of so-called *Weltalter* drafts (1811–15), which are an attempted summary of his early thought. As Žižek writes, the usual understanding of Schelling is that he stands against the Absolute Idealism of Hegel, introducing 'a gap which opens a way for the post-Hegelian problematic of finitude' (*IR*, 5–6). It is a reading that obviously leads to Heidegger, who in fact proposed something similar in his *Schelling's Treatise on the Essence of Human Freedom*. Žižek, however, contests this interpretation of Schelling and Hegel, this 'formal envelope of error' (*IR*, 6) that would construct both in this way. Rather, if Schelling relates to Hegel, it is not in *opposing* him but in bringing out something that is already in him. That is, after Schelling, it is possible to read Hegel as a philosopher not of Absolute Knowledge but of the *failure* of Absolute Knowledge; the dialectic not as the reconciliation of opposites or the negation of the world but as the 'negation of negation': the proposing not of some alternative to the world but the thinking of what is excluded from it to ensure it is the way it is. To put it in terms of the vanishing mediator, we might say that Hegel is not a great Enlightenment philosopher but the first great post-Enlightenment philosopher; that there is no going beyond Hegel, that we can henceforth only repeat him – but all this only *after* Schelling.

More specifically – as part of this complicated thinking of finitude – Žižek takes up the central problem Schelling grappled with throughout his career, and especially in the various *Weltalter* drafts (of which there are three successive versions). It can be stated, following Žižek, as the very problem of *beginning*, of how the world came into being (*IR*, 13). How is the world created? By what series of actions did it become real? But this can also be understood in terms of the post-Kantian problematic of freedom. By what act or resolution did God create the world? What is the status of His decision to bring the world about? Now, of course, a well-known series of philosophical difficulties is raised by our attempt to think this primordial act. First of all, given that it precedes the symbolic order, how could we know of it? How could this God be disclosed to us and perhaps even to Himself (*IR*, 14)? But, second and more profoundly, how in a world governed by natural laws are we to explain a

decision like this? Is it an act outside of time that suspends or even precedes the laws of causality? If so, how is it able to act upon the world?
If not, in what sense can it be free (*IR*, 16)? And, again, what would be
the status of God before His decision to begin the world? Does He simply
pre-exist the world? Or does He come into being with it? In that case,
who exactly makes the decision to begin the world? These are the deadlocks that have long bedevilled the notion of any founding act or
unmoved mover, which always seems to shift between the alternatives
of temporal/eternal, free/determined and phenomenal/noumenal. And
the entire aim of post-Kantian philosophy – from Hegel to Schelling to
Derrida to Žižek – has been how to 'reconcile' these alternatives, how
to think them together.

How then does Schelling aim to resolve these deadlocks? The decisive
aspect of his approach – and it is this, according to Žižek, that makes
him a materialist and not an idealist – is that he reverses the usual
terms of the problem. It is not for him a matter of how God's freedom
arises or is to be explained within an already existing world of causal
necessity. Rather, the question is: how does this series of connections
arise in the first place? What is that act which allows this symbolic
order to start at all (*IR*, 16)? And yet – this undoubtedly in response to
objections to the status of God before this act – it is also true that this
decision or act by God is not literally the first thing, that the 'true Beginning is not at the beginning' (*IR*, 13). That is, 'before' God's initial decision – but, of course, it is precisely the meaning of this 'before' that is in
question here – there is not so much the usual theological eternity, from
which God falls with His decision into time, as what Žižek calls the
'chaotic-psychotic universe of the blind drives, their rotary motion,
their undifferentiated pulsating' (*IR*, 13). But what exactly is this
'rotary motion', and how might it allow us to avoid the usual dilemmas
attending the notion of the birth of the world? Žižek describes it, following Schelling, in terms of an alternating 'contraction' and 'expansion'.
In his words, in a first moment of 'contraction', a pure potentiality of
freedom which is complete and wants for nothing 'actualizes itself
in the guise of a will which actually, effectively wants this "nothing"'
(*IR*, 23). Then, in a second moment of 'expansion', after experiencing
itself as negation and destruction, this will opposes or reverses itself in
the guise of a will that now wants 'something' (*IR*, 23). And yet, as
Žižek makes clear, both of these moments miss their mark. They are
either too much or not enough. A cycle of 'contraction' can only be followed by one of 'expansion', and vice versa. A proper 'balance' is unable

to be struck. The more God attempts to actualize the world, the more He realizes there is to do. The faster He attempts to run, the further He understands there is to go. A little like Zeno's paradoxes of motion, we can never really explain how the world begins at all, how God makes any progress. As Žižek writes: 'God repeatedly dashes Himself against His own wall: unable to stay within, He follows His urge to break out, yet the more He struggles to escape, the more He is caught in His own trap' (*IR*, 23).[4]

It is this cycle that is broken by a *decision* – a decision that, as Žižek says, finally 'contracts' this rotary drive and takes us back to an ' "absolute indifference" *qua* the abyss of pure freedom' (*IR*, 14). But, in his language here, Žižek again comes very close to that first moment of 'rotary motion'. So what is the difference? How is the act, though close to rotary motion, and perhaps drawing on its energies, not quite the same as it? Why do we not, after this 'contradiction', simply go back to another cycle of 'expansion', and so on? To begin to answer these questions, we might translate these two moments back into what we have previously spoken of with regard to the symbolic order. 'Contraction', that moment when the free, untethered will actualizes itself in the guise of a will that wills 'nothing', is equivalent to that first 're-marking' of the void, the primordial division of a thing from itself. 'Expansion' is the moment of the naming of this 'nothing', of having something stand in for it. And we can see here that Schelling's thinking of the act or decision that breaks the 'rotary cycle' repeats the logic of 'concrete universality', in which the void directly coincides with its naming, at once is opened up and closed by its being named. That is, what is at stake in this decision is not so much an 'alternation' between contraction and expansion as the *simultaneity* between the two. We can always imagine each statement of the 'empty' master-signifier turning into a 'something', and this something in turn revealing that 'nothing' that stands behind it. But Žižek through his rethinking of Schelling wants to break with this 'bad infinity', which still implicitly resorts to a model of a potential becoming actual (it is as though each time it is a matter either of filling up or exposing a prior emptiness), and imagine instead, like that figure of the king we have looked at before (*IR*, 87), an immediate *equivalence* between a thing and its opposite (in which to expose emptiness *is* to fill it in, in which to fill it in *is* to expose it).

It is something like this simultaneity that Žižek attempts to think in *Indivisible Remainder* in terms of the relationship of the act to its 'ground'. What is the ground of the act? As we know, the act is not primordial. It intervenes in an already existing situation; it is undertaken on the basis of certain reasons. And the ground might be defined as just that variety of factors, both objective and subjective, that any act seeks to take into account. It is these that we might say it 'contracts', in the sense of summarizing, condensing, abstracting, in order to draw some consequence or conclusion from them. That is, the act 'contracts' the ground, not only in the legal sense that it becomes responsible for it but, as in something like Nietzsche's Eternal Return, in the sense that it repeats it, assumes it, binds itself to it (*IR*, 132). And yet, as Žižek also emphasizes, Schelling's thought is not a form of *Lebensphilosophie*: it is not a matter of any immersion in some substantial life-substance; this ground that precedes the act is not material but thoroughly logical (*IR*, 28). Rather, if what precedes the act is a ground, this ground does not exist before the act. As we know from our ordinary thinking, if in one way we seek to justify our behaviour by reference to some prior set of conditions, in another way these conditions would not have any relevance until they were 'taken on' by our act. Again, the complicated point that Schelling is trying to think via his notion of 'rotary motion' is that at once the act is not before the ground and the ground is not before the act. Although there is nothing outside of the act, it is nevertheless not performatively complete, entirely able to account for itself. Although it will inevitably lead to that master-signifier that justifies it, from which nothing is left out, all of this is only possible because of a certain ground (in a sense, precisely the 'act' itself).[5] What Žižek is trying to speak of in this relationship between the act and the ground is not so much an act outside or before its ground as that 'act' left out at that moment when the act becomes the ground, that 'act' that allows the transformation of the act into a master-signifier. What he is trying to think, to use his own expression, is the act as the very 'becoming' of the master-signifier.

Can we put all this another way? How does this actually play itself out in more detail in Schelling's philosophy? Schelling, in fact, extraordinarily enough, provides in one of his *Weltalter* drafts a so-called 'formula of the world'. It goes:

$$\left(\frac{A^3}{A^2 = (A = B)} \right) B$$

which Žižek describes as showing how the 'ever-increasing "sublation [*Aufhebung*]" of the Real (B) in the Ideal (A), the progressive subordination of the Real to the Ideal, relies on the exception of a B which, as the excluded ground of the process of sublation, guarantees its consistency' (*IR*, 77). He then goes on to specify:

The crucial aspect not to be missed is the *self-relating* character of this repetition: when a given relationship between the two poles (between 'A' and 'B', the ideal and real pole) is raised to a higher power, one of the two poles is posited as the form, the neutral medium, of the new, higher polarity . . . It is because of this self-referentiality that we are dealing here not with the same form repeating itself in different material domains, but with an incessant interchange between form and content: part of the content of a lower level becomes the formal principle of a higher level. (*IR*, 56)

What we have here is the idea that it is the ground of the act (B) that keeps on being contracted or sublated to be turned into a figure (A), but this only to produce, this only to leave out, another B. That is, each equivalence of A = B as a numerator is underpinned by B as a denominator; and this occurs each time this B is shown to be equivalent to A. Thus that B to the right of the equation is the ground that allows the passage of that B into A to its left, which is the ground that allows the A^2 to its left, which is the ground that allows the A^3 above it. But again, crucially, this B does not exist before being stood in for, comes about only as an effect of something taking its place. It is only what allows A or what is retrospectively seen as a result of A. And, of course, this idea of something both being and not being part of itself (B as at once what is equal to A and what is excluded to allow A) brings us back to what we said about enunciation in Chapter 1 and antagonism in Chapter 2. It should also remind us of what we said earlier about Benjamin's messianic conception of history, for in a similar way – and *Indivisible Remainder* explicitly makes the connection in terms of a past that never was (*IR*, 21–2) – it is the same ground or past 'in itself' that is continually being requilted there. That is, what Schelling is trying to speak of in his 'formula of the world' – as Benjamin with that future that allows the 'continuum' between past and present – is that point B that produces the equivalence between figure and ground, A and B. However, as soon as it is named, we lose it. It becomes equivalent only to 'A'; its 'nothing' turns into something. We are unable to speak of this point without it being 're-marked', without something standing in for it; but this point does not exist before being stood in for, it exists only as its loss. And *this* is how Schelling's 'formula' captures life, how his 'system' takes off: it is not a matter of an act before a ground or a ground before its act, but both are born at once and the process never comes to an end.

To say all this again more slowly, as Schelling argues – and this is the real meaning of 'finitude' in philosophy; this is why Schelling is a post-Enlightenment philosopher – the true task of philosophy is indeed a kind of 'contraction'. Its aim is not critically to filter out reality, select between competing alternatives, directly imagine that things could be otherwise – Schelling breaks with this fundamentally Leibnizian conception (*K*, 81) – but simply to accept, affirm, what is. This is also, as we have seen, Žižek's conception of philosophy's relationship to what comes before it: that each successive philosophical system does not refute the system before, adduce evidence against it, but goes to the very ends of its premises, pushes it to its furthest extent. But, again, in this very re-marking of what is, a certain space is opened up, which Žižek calls 'transcendental' (*TN*, 3). It is a space at once outside of the system before, which it is unaware of, and inside this system, which allows it to be complete, to require no other. This system is only able to be constituted from the point of view of a certain 'nothing', which becomes a 'something' in the system which 're-marks' it, and which in turn allows another to 're-mark' that 'nothing' which makes *it* possible, and so on. In a sense, we are always either too soon or too late for this ground; it is always not yet or already re-marked – but what we are trying to capture is precisely the equivalence of A and B, figure and ground, enunciated and enunciation. However, this could only ever be done from another, 'higher' ground; this could only leave out another ground. This is why we might call this ground not so much 'transcendental' as 'proto-transcendental' (*L*, 279): at once more transcendental than transcendental, what allows any 'transcendental' to be named, and less than transcendental, showing that any such 'transcendental' is only able to be named in terms of the system it apparently explains, is made possible by another.

To return once more to the subject of this chapter: all of this is exactly like the relationship of the act to the master-signifier. The act is only a master-signifier, can only become a master-signifier (just as B can only become A); but this only because of a certain 'act' that opens up the symbolic order and for which this symbolic order stands in. And yet, if this 'act' initiates the symbolic order, it cannot be seen outside of it, is a 'failure' that can only be expressed in terms of it. It is for this reason that Žižek in *Indivisible Remainder* connects these meditations by Schelling on the beginning of the world to Lacan's notoriously difficult 'formulae of sexuation' (*IR*, 155–61). It is to speak of the way that, throughout Žižek's work (or gradually imposing itself upon it), the act is not to be thought of as a masculine 'exception' to the symbolic order but, in a 'feminine' way, as that which makes it 'not-all'. That is, the act does not stand outside of the symbolic order – for there is nothing outside of the symbolic order; it is just this that means there is nothing outside of the symbolic order – but introduces a kind of 'split' within it. It does not oppose to things some unfulfilled potential or some 'progressive' or even 'revolutionary' cause. Rather, if we can say this, the act introduces a split *between things and themselves*. It is not a matter of some distinction between the exception and the norm, or even between part and whole; but the very thing that allows the world to be all that is the case, to form a universal, is a certain space outside of it, which inverts or negates it. To put this another way, what Žižek says he sees in the 'feminine' – and this should remind us of the relationship between A and B in Schelling's 'formula of the world' – is the collapse between 'function and meta-function' (*IR*, 157). The same element that allows us to speak of the world is subject to the world; what frames ends up being framed. And this will lead in Žižek's later work to what he calls the 'sinthome' or 'universal symptom' (*T?*, 100). It is a state of generalized perversion or psychosis in which any exception to the symbolic order is impossible, but only because the whole system is already made up of nothing but exceptions; each element in the chain of equivalents attempts to be the key to the entire symbolic order, and therefore none is. What is the possibility of the 'act' in such circumstances – which are precisely those of today's 'postmodern' society – when there is nothing left to transgress or when transgression becomes the norm? What of the 'act' is not given here, even though it appears to be occurring all of the time? (And, of course, Žižek's own analysis comes close to this, in that it too is able to find the key to the whole system of contemporary capitalism in any of its 'idiotic details' [*ME*, 175].)

So how, then, to think of the 'act' today? What is the difference between Žižek's analysis and that postmodern condition he describes? It is at this point that we return to an extremely complex point in Schelling that is raised by thinking of the act in terms of these 'formulae of sexuation', and that is dealt with perhaps a little too quickly by Žižek. We might start with that question we began by asking here: what is the real difference between the act or decision and that endless cycle of 'rotary motion' it breaks with? With regard to rotary motion, we spoke of the way that in it there is an *opposition* between contraction and expansion. But we cannot thereby explain how it actually begins – or it would remain in a 'steady state' in which nothing changes – because, in so far as the ground (expansion) is understood to be the external limit to the figure (contraction), we would have to imagine that, even if not now, at some time in the future, this ground will run out: there will be no more ground to contract. Paradoxically, it is only in so far as the very turning of the ground into a figure produces or requires another ground that we can imagine the world beginning and not coming to a halt. Here the process does not end, things change, though not in the simple evolutionary sense of a transformation from a potential to an actual, but as a constant 'raising to a higher power', an endless series of *doublings* (in which at the same time nothing changes, the world as such never becomes more 'advanced'). It is what we might call *drive* as opposed to rotary motion. But – and this is the most complicated point of all, taking us back to the fall of the 'binary signifier' in Chapter 1 and the question of the 'two limits' we will see in Žižek's dispute with Butler and Laclau in Chapter 5 – if it is this *simultaneity* of contraction and expansion, nothing and something, the void and what stands in for it, that is at stake here, this simultaneity is also impossible. We can only ever have either one or the other: the void before what fills it in or what fills it in revealing the void. That is – and this perhaps explains the failure of each of Schelling's *Weltalter* drafts, with each attempting to resolve differently this impossible simultaneity – it is not a matter of *opposing* rotary motion, for we can only ever think in terms of it. And it is not even a matter of not thinking in terms of the exception, of an act that is marked out from the rest of the field. Rather, the true paradox – the meaning of Žižek's insistence on the existence of the act when there is no actual act – is that, if Žižek chooses one element or example to represent the whole system, this is only to show the *impossibility* of any such exception. This is why it always remains a question of *choice*, of an *act* (of some named object), even though this is only to point to what cannot be named, to speak of something that has not yet taken place. It is why, as we will see in the next chapter, Žižek's politics are ultimately those of *contingency*: how his analysis has to proceed through a certain suspension of disbelief, the fact that, to paraphrase him, he 'knows very well what he is doing, but nevertheless he is still doing it' (*SO*, 29).[6]

Badiou

Žižek develops many of these ideas later in *Ticklish Subject*. The book is first of all an argument for the continued relevance of the 'subject' in contemporary politics and thought – the subject in the sense of that 'split subject' we have been trying to elaborate throughout – but one of its other long-running themes is the notion of the symbolic order standing in for some prior act. It is something that obviously comes out of his previous work on Schelling, although it is not always stated as doing so.

We might trace just one aspect of this here. Žižek in *Ticklish Subject* argues that the Sublime does not indicate, through its failure to be thought, some noumenal Reason, but rather suggests the very failure of Reason itself: 'The Sublime, in its extreme, in its approaching the monstrous, indicates an abyss which is already concealed, "gentrified", by the Ideas of Reason' (*TS*, 39). This will lead him to make a distinction between Kant and Hegel: that whereas in Kant the Sublime hints at another, noumenal dimension, an exception to Reason (masculine), in Hegel it is just what allows the phenomenal and Reason as such, thus rendering them 'not-all' (feminine). A connection is then made to that 'uncanny X that precedes transcendentally constituted reality' (*TS*, 55) that Heidegger points to in his criticism of Kant's two *Critiques* in his *Kant and the Problem of Metaphysics*, which we have called the 'quasi-transcendental'. Finally, Žižek joins this sublime 'free act' that posits reality and Benjamin's messianic vision of history: 'The excess/lack [of revolutionary potential] is not part of the "objective" that is in excess of the subject's cognitive capacities: rather, it consists of the traces of the subject himself (his crushed hopes and desires) in the object' (*TS*, 89–90). That is, we can now see that the revolutionary potential/split in the past, the one thing that cannot be accounted for, is the very decision by the subject to look back into history to construct it in their image (a look back which can only see this revolutionary potential as lost). It is the very subject looking back bringing about this irreversible condition that itself introduces a split into the past.

It is this Hegelian anti-Kantianism, this thinking of the act in terms not of the exception but the not-all, that can be seen in *Ticklish Subject* through Žižek's treatment of the contemporary French political philosopher Alain Badiou in the chapter 'The Politics of Truth'. Žižek in principle approves of Badiou – consistent with his own anti-deconstructionist stance – because, to put it crudely (and both Žižek and Badiou *can* be crude in their characterization of deconstruction), Badiou restores the notion of 'Truth'. Badiou attacks deconstruction for its ultimately 'commonsensical' notion that the Truth is too complex to be known entirely (*TS*, 133). As Žižek writes:

> One can readily grasp the gap that separates Badiou from deconstructionist fictionalism: his radical opposition to the idea of a 'multitude of truths' (or, rather, 'truth-effects'). Truth is contingent; it hinges on a concrete historical situation; it is the truth of this situation, but in every concrete and contingent historical situation there is *one and only one* Truth which, once articulated,

spoken out, functions as the index of itself and of the falsity of the field subverted by it. (*TS*, 131)

On the contrary, it is the infinite 'complexity' argued for by Derrida that would prevent the possibility of this 'speaking out': like the necessity of the noumenal remaining unknowable if we wish to remain free, so for Derrida the act can never be definitively accomplished. As with Kant on the French Revolution, there is in Derrida an enthusiasm for the act as Idea, along with a suspicion of those who actually carry it out. It is, in the end, a hysterical refusal of the reality of the act and its consequences. For Derrida, according to Badiou, there must always remain a gap between us and the act (*TS*, 133–4).

What, then, would be the contrary Truth or Truth-Event for Badiou? It is close to what we have spoken of before with regard to Schelling. As with the founding act or decision in him, the Truth is what reveals the void for which the existing situation stands in. It is what takes the place of what is excluded to make the current symbolic order possible. As Žižek says, summarizing Badiou, it emerges *ex nihilo* and attaches itself to the 'void of every situation, to its inherent inconsistency and/or its excess. The Event is the Truth of the situation that makes visible/legible what the "official" situation had to "repress" ' (*TS*, 130). Thus, to take some examples, the French Revolution makes clear the censorship and repression that kept the reigning monarchy in power. The Russian Revolution brings out the economic exploitation that underpinned Tsarism. But, again, this void is not visible – in Badiou's words, not 'proper', not 'countable' (*TS*, 129) – before this Truth-Event. As we have already seen with the act, it is not merely a matter of seeing some absence or ambiguity in the previous order and then deciding to move. Rather, it is the very act itself that leads to this absence. This is precisely the self-fulfilling or performative nature of the act or Truth-Event. The reasons for it cannot be seen within the existing symbolic horizon, but only by those already involved in it. (Badiou/Žižek's favourite example of this is the French historian François Furet's explaining away of the French Revolution as merely a series of unrelated incidents that do not add up to anything, whereas for those caught up in them these same occurrences take on an entirely meaningful unity and consistency [*TS*, 136].) And, following this, the task of those loyal to the Cause represented by the Event, in an unapologetic dogmatism, is to be faithful to its Truth, to seek to develop or explicate all of its consequences. As Žižek writes: 'What defines the subject is his fidelity to the Event: the subject comes after the Event and persists in discerning its traces within his situation' (*TS*, 130).

This idea of a Truth-Event attaching itself to a situation, bringing out that void against which its 'order' can be seen, is obviously very close to Žižek. And yet he ultimately disagrees with it. What, then, is the difference between Badiou's conception of the Truth-Event and Žižek's of the act? What is the source of that distinction that Žižek seeks to make between them? On the one hand, Žižek agrees with Badiou: the undecidability/void of the previous situation does not exist until it has been drawn attention to by a subsequent act. As with Benjamin, we never actually have that void or alternative as such; it exists only in retrospect, as the very effect of its loss: 'The status of the pure multiple and its void is also undecidable and purely "intermediary": we never encounter it "now", since it is always recognized as such retrospectively, through the act of Decision that dissolves it' (*TS*, 137–8). And yet, if this void is only ever virtual, a retrospective effect of its naming, it is not simply the same as its master-signifier. If we do not always miss the event, as with Derrida, it is also not a matter of directly identifying with it, as with Badiou. This is what distinguishes Žižek's/Lacan's position from Badiou's. For Badiou, this opening up of the void is inseparable from the master-signifier that sutures it: 'The gesture that closes/decides the Situation (again) thus absolutely coincides with the gesture that (retroactively) opens it up' (*TS*, 138). For Žižek, on the other hand, the interpretive intervention – the act – say, of psychoanalysis does not posit a new symbolic order, a new Truth-Event. It rather wipes the slate clean in preparation for one. As he writes:

> For Lacan, negativity, a negative gesture of withdrawal, precedes any positive gesture of enthusiastic identification with a Cause: negativity functions as the condition of (im)possibility of the enthusiastic identification – that is to say, it lays the ground, opens up space for it, but is simultaneously obfuscated by it and undermines it. (*TS*, 154)

As we can see from this passage, however, the distinction at stake here is much more complicated than the simple assertion of a 'prior' negativity in Lacan as opposed to a negativity that arises only in retrospect in Badiou. As Žižek admits, even with Lacan, this void is not entirely unattached to the master-signifier, but at once makes it 'possible' and is 'obfuscated' by it. So, again, what *is* the difference between them?

In fact, Žižek makes another, perhaps unexpected criticism of Badiou. We have previously seen him hold Badiou up against the 'Kantianism' of Derrida and his notion of some 'sublime' event that can never be actualized or ontologized. And, against this, he has juxtaposed Badiou's absolute identification of the Event with its naming. But we can also see Žižek accusing Badiou of thinking in terms of the same Kantian 'betrayal' of the act (*TS*, 159), the same necessity to distinguish between acts and pseudo-acts (*TS*, 128), the same endless doubts as to whether an act has been given its proper name (*L*, 272), and even of repeating a pre-Pauline circularity between the law and its transgression (*TS*, 150–51), so much like that rotary motion we looked at before.[7] How is this so? Why is there this problem in Badiou? It is because, even though he speaks of the void of a situation only being revealed by its subsequent master-signifier or Truth-Event, this void is still seen as logically prior to it. This is why any relationship to this void is always haunted by the possibility of betrayal, why any subjective identification with this void always risks 'ontologizing' both the subject and the void (*TS*, 159). It is to continue to understand this void as an *exception*, as what breaks with or stands outside of the symbolic order. And it is to persist in understanding any subjective action or decision as occurring only within an already constituted symbolic order, as an anomaly within that order, as opposed to the Schellingian–Hegelian idea that this whole order and its corollary of freedom are only possible because of some prior 'act' or 'decision'.

What is this 'subject' over which Žižek and Badiou dispute? For Žižek at least, it would not be a subject that is faithful to some (pre-existing) Cause, but a subject that *is* a Cause (if Badiou speaks in terms of a certain interpellation by this Cause, the relationship Žižek is imagining is much closer). As he writes:

> Identifying the subject with the constitutive void of the structure – such an identification already 'ontologizes' the subject, albeit in a purely negative way – that is, it turns the subject into an entity entirely consubstantial with the structure, an entity that belongs to the order of what is necessary and a priori ('no structure without a subject'). (*TS*, 159)

And this language should remind us of Schellingian 'contraction': it is not here so much a prior void or Cause with which the subject identifies – or which is revealed, as in certain readings of the Sublime, by our inability to grasp it – as one that comes about only because of the subject, because of our subjective identification with it. The entire symbolic order stands in for this subject; but this subject would also not exist before this standing in. And this is the true meaning of that *simultaneity* of the void and the master-signifier that Žižek opposes to Badiou: it is not a matter of a void or event that occurs *within* the symbolic order, but a void or event that *is* the symbolic order, that drives the infinite expansion of the symbolic order in making of it a 'not-all'. And it is in this sense that we must understand that 'circularity' of the subject forever trying to catch up with itself that Žižek speaks of in *Ticklish Subject* and elsewhere (*TS*, 159; *TN*, 171). It is not simply some 'rotary motion', in which an already constituted subject either takes on or fights against its symbolic identification, which as we have seen is only that 'inherent transgression' necessary for the Symbolic. (It is this position that Žižek compares to that dialectic of the law and its transgression that St Paul breaks with and that Badiou still repeats.) Rather, it is a matter of a 'not-all' subject that at the very moment of its symbolic identification leaves out that subjective act that makes this possible. It is a question not of the subject versus the Symbolic but of the subject versus the subject; not of some subjective identification with the Symbolic (including any so-called Truth-Effect) but of the subject itself as Cause (the subject as that split or lack that any such Truth-Effect arises in response to, attempts to take the place of) (*TS*, 159).

Indeed, another name for this 'circularity' or 'cycle' is the *death-drive*. That is, the death-drive is to be understood not as any end-point or even negativity, but as a form of immortal life: the death-drive is what always comes back to mark itself as absent. And this drive can be seen in all of those great ethical characters that Žižek speaks of throughout his work – Oedipus at Colonnus, Antigone, Sygne de Coûfontaine, even Lacan – who refuse to compromise their desire, who keep on insisting on their original position, no matter how circumstances change, no matter who is against them (*TS*, 154–5, 160–61). But, crucially, they are able to keep on coming back in this way, not because there is something still left to be done – again, this is not at all to be understood in terms of some potential becoming actual – but because it is their attempt to accomplish their goal that leads to what needs to be done, because they are themselves the disturbance they seek to make right. These figures testify to the 'death-drive', but this death-drive is not something beyond but only something seen through (the failure of) the act.[8] The 'death-drive' – symbolic withdrawal – is a 'precondition' of the act, but it cannot be grasped outside of it, arises only as an effect of it (otherwise we would reduce it to merely another symbolic identification statable in advance, a Cause that can only inevitably be compromised). More subtly perhaps, Žižek is not directly opposed to Badiou's 'Truth-Event' or Cause as exception, but wants to think what allows it, not in the sense of being the 'transcendental' condition of it, but as something that at once initiates it and can only be seen through it (again, it might be thought in terms of a kind of Hegelian Sublime or Derridean 'quasi-transcendental'). As Žižek writes:

> In this precise sense, the act involves a dimension of death-drive that grounds a decision (to accomplish a hegemonic identification; to engage in a fidelity to a Truth), but cannot be reduced to it. The Lacanian death-drive (a category Badiou adamantly opposes) is thus again a kind of 'vanishing-mediator' between Being and Event: there is a 'negative' gesture constitutive of the subject which is then obfuscated in 'Being' (the established ontological order) and in fidelity to the Event. (*TS*, 160)

This assertion of a certain 'minimal distance' between the death-drive and what stands in for it, between the 'negative gesture of suspension-withdrawal-contradiction and the positive gesture of filling its void' (*TS*, 160), has ethical consequences for Žižek. First of all, it is to insist that the (symbolic dimension of the) Truth-Event is not final or definitive: that 'prior' to the Truth-Event is that 'gap' or 'void' that renders it at once possible and impossible, that 'opens up and sustains the space for the Truth-Event, yet its excess always threatens to undermine it' (*TS*, 161). And, for Žižek, although the attempt to speak for this dimension inevitably runs the risk of a Kantian *Schwärmerei* or belief in a direct fusion with a mystical 'beyond', it is also only this dimension that ensures any true ethics, makes possible the incessant questioning of any proposed Truth-Event or master-signifier. As he says, the true calamities of the twentieth century (from the Holocaust to Stalinism) have resulted not from succumbing to the lure of the beyond but from refusing to confront it (*TS*, 161). It is this questioning that Žižek characterizes as the attitude of the Analyst as opposed to the (Badiouian) Master, always maintaining the 'simultaneous necessity and impossibility (ultimate failure) of [the Event's] symbolization' (*TS*, 165). But, again, as with the gap of 'withdrawal', the ultimate status of this 'beyond' requires explanation – it is this that will give us a clue as to how Žižek can avoid the temptation of some direct access to the noumenal Thing. For Žižek, this 'beyond' is not simply outside or before or even the retrospective effect of the master-signifier, as it is for Badiou. Rather, it *is* the master-signifier, what arises *at the same time* as the master-signifier. For Badiou, that is, there is ultimately a limit to any symbolic naming and, in a Kantian way, this means that we should never really try to name the Truth (*TS*, 166–7). But, as with Kant – this is Hegel's well-known critique – Badiou could no sooner say what this exception is than he would have to name it himself, thus overstepping the very limit he warns against (this is in fact the circularity between the law and its transgression that St Paul diagnoses): the community in politics, sexual *jouissance* in love, beauty in art … (*TS*, 167). For Žižek, the only way to avoid both this sublime unnameability and its eventual betrayal is to state that the only thing that cannot be named is the *act* itself, that which allows all else to be named. As Žižek writes: 'So – to put it succinctly – for Lacan, the authentic act itself in its negative dimension, the act as the Real of an "object" preceding naming, is what is ultimately *innomable*' (*TS*, 167).

Žižek can thus be seen to be attempting to 'mediate' between Derrida and Badiou: between the act as deferred and unattainable and the act as existing only within the Symbolic; between a void that precedes and is outside of the Symbolic and a void that is merely a retrospective effect of the Symbolic. Against both of these alternatives, as we have tried to show, Žižek seeks to think the *simultaneity* of the act and the void, the master-signifier and *object a*. And yet we can wonder whether Žižek does not himself at times make the same mistakes of which he accuses others; whether in a typical Žižekian manner the person he is fundamentally arguing against is himself. For we might say that Žižek remains profoundly Kantian in continuing to maintain – perhaps in slightly different terms – a distinction between an order of positive knowledge of Being and a wholly different Truth-Event (*TS*, 166). We can wonder whether, for all of Žižek's talk of a void that at once makes possible and impossible, allows and is obfuscated by, the act, there is not still a certain distinction made between them. That is, when Žižek speaks of the 'primacy of the (negative) act over the (positive) establishment of a "new harmony" via the intervention of some new master-signifier' (*TS*, 159), how are we to understand this? Or the act as a 'reference to the void at its core, prior to filling in this void' (*TS*, 160)? Or, indeed, the 'minimal distance' between the 'negative gesture of suspension-withdrawal-contraction and the positive gesture of filling its void' (*TS*, 160)? Does this primacy or gap indicate some logical or temporal succession or cause, with the void coming before and leading to its filling in, or is it the 'gap' of the death-drive (*TS*, 165), so much like the 'enchainment' (*IR*, 56) or 'undecidability' (*IR*, 29) of those two poles in Schelling? Is all this simply the result of the difficulty of expressing simultaneity, the paradox of two different things being present at the same time? And, although this might appear a mere quibble, everything, up to God Himself, depends on it, from the exact meaning of saying that the act occurs 'between' two deaths (*SO*, 134–6; *TS*, 152–8) to the idea that there are two distinct 'moments' in the act, one occurring within the existing symbolic order and the other a resignifying of this order (*TS*, 72; *CHU*, 108–12); and on to the notion that there are two traumas, one intrapsychic and ahistorical and the other real and historical (*FA*, 92–4). Again, the question to be resolved – through the slow, patient elaboration of Žižek's text – is whether in each case Žižek is suggesting a temporal/logical distinction between the two levels, in which case he falls into just those difficulties he so brilliantly diagnoses in Derrida and Badiou, or whether he is attempting to break down their opposition, with the ultimate impossibility of doing so within the symbolic order, in the same way that we can only ever grasp the founding 'Event' in the form of a 'fantasy' (*FA*, 73). We will return to these questions in Chapter 4, which both attempts to make this relationship between the master-signifier and *object a* clearer and is the third failed attempt, after the two previous chapters, to do so.

Chapter 4

The 'negation of negation'

At the end of the last chapter, we considered a number of examples of a *gap* between the empirical and the transcendental in Žižek's work: between actual and symbolic death; between contingent trauma and the deeper trauma for which it stands in; between the negation that occurs within the symbolic order and the negation that founds the symbolic order. It is a gap that Žižek insists on maintaining, on keeping open. In *Contingency, Hegemony, Universality*, he speaks of the importance of distinguishing between the universality within which ideological struggles take place and the exclusion that allows this empty place: So Lacan is the very opposite of Kantian formalism (if by this we understand the imposition of some formal frame that serves as the a priori of its contingent content): Lacan forces us to make thematic the exclusion of some traumatic 'content' that is constitutive of the empty, universal form. (*CHU*, 111)

In *Plague of Fantasies*, he warns of the potential psychosis that results from the bringing together of the Symbolic and the Real in such things as computer games: 'As has often been said, Virtual Reality is a kind of Orwellian misnomer. What is threatened in its rise is the very dimension of virtuality consubstantial with the symbolic order' (*PF*, 155). And in *Fragile Absolute*, he welcomes the attempts of contemporary artists to keep this space open by elevating ordinary objects to this Sacred Place: 'It is today's artists who display excremental objects who, far from undermining the logic of [symbolic] sublimation, are desperately trying to save it' (*FA*, 32).

All of this is not unrelated to that other 'gap' we see in Žižek, which occurs in the form of questions like: is it the Real that arises in response to some impasse in the Symbolic or is it the Symbolic that arises in response to some deadlock in the Real? It is the first option that Žižek regards as idealist, and the second that he regards as materialist

(*FA*, 91–2). Thus, in *Indivisible Remainder*, he is able to argue against the French literary theorist Jean-Jacques Lecercle for the priority of *lalangue* (language in its meaningless, asignifying dimension) over the Big Other (language as symbolic order): 'Lacan repeatedly asserted the *jouis-sense* of the letter as a kind of base out of which, via the operation of phallic exclusion ("symbolic castration"), the discursive order of the Big Other emerges' (*IR*, 109). In *Fragile Absolute*, he is similarly able to argue that all representations of the Real only shield us from it, miss its traumatic impact: 'The images of utter catastrophe, far from giving access to the Real, can function as a protective shield *against* the Real' (*FA*, 78). And, in *For They Know Not*, he will argue that the symbolic order as such is nothing but the response to some underlying trauma, the attempt to make up for some prior unsymbolizable Real:

> The most famous case of such retroactive causality within the field of psychoanalysis is of course that of the 'Wolf Man', Freud's Russian analysand who as a child witnessed the parental *coitus a tergo*: all his later symptom-formations were nothing but so many endeavours to integrate this primal scene into the present, synchronous symbolic network, to confer meaning upon it and thus to contain its traumatic impact. (*TK*, 202)

These passages are undoubtedly more complex than we have allowed; and it is certainly possible to contend that elsewhere (and even in these passages) Žižek is arguing *against* the simple alternative between the Symbolic and the Real that seems to be played out in them. Nevertheless, we would say that, in continuing to draw a distinction between the Symbolic and the Real – in suggesting that a void exists prior to being filled in, that it is an impasse in the Real that leads to the Symbolic, that the Real is gentrified by the Symbolic – Žižek risks being *Kantian*. We would say that, despite his brilliant critique of Badiou and Derrida, he perhaps repeats the very same 'formalism' as them. That is, what Žižek fails to grasp in these passages is that the Symbolic *is* the Real, that the void does *not* exist before being filled in, that the Real *cannot* by definition be lost or 'gentrified'. And this is what is meant by the Hegelian notion of the 'negation of negation', which is the subject of this chapter and our third attempt to speak of the relationship between the master-signifier and the act. What is the 'negation of negation'? It is the idea that, if the act can be considered a 'negation' of the master-signifier, this 'negation' must itself be 'negated', shown to be part of the master-signifier. And yet, if this 'negation of negation' means that nothing is outside of the master-signifier, it also allows us to think that this master-signifier is not all, that it is only possible as the 'negation' of the 'negation' of the act. This is 'negation of negation' as what we might call the 'loss of loss' (*CHU*, 258): at once there is no loss, no other to the system, and there is a loss even beyond loss, a loss that any actual loss can only stand in for. It is an act that is not opposed to the system, for it could only be that 'inherent transgression' that allows it (*ME*, 55–7; *PF*, 18–27; *CHU*, 218–19), but that *is* the system. It is the system itself and its endless ability to appropriate the act that is only possible as the 'normalization' (*TS*, 183) or 'positivization' (*TS*, 234) of some prior 'act'.

This rethinking of the act in turn leads to a certain reconceptualization of the bases for ethical and political action. In doing away with the notion of the act as some exception to the existing order, Žižek does away with the Enlightenment idea of action as guided by some goal to be attained in the future. Rather, the 'quasi-transcendental' conditions of possibility – this gap or negation we have been speaking of – would lie not elsewhere but *here*. It would be a matter not so much of changing the world into something else as of making the world the way it *already is*. It would be not so much a matter of opposing an other to the world as of showing that the world is already its own other, possible only on the basis of a split that occurred before it was born. (Žižek's distinction here is between the thinking of a pseudo-messianic future that will never arrive and a catastrophe that has already happened [*TS*, 71; *B*, 125].) And this will lead to a certain reconceptualization by Žižek of the notion of the social or political *Cause*, that for which we struggle and die. For, along the lines of this doing away with the act as 'negation', Žižek also wants to do away with the usual ways of understanding Cause. He wants to get rid of both the idea of the Cause as a fantasy untouched by reality (*T?*, 111–12) and the idea that the Cause is always compromised by reality (*TS*, 165). Indeed, corresponding with a certain shift of allegiance from Antigone to Medea, Žižek will ultimately come to reject the whole idea of the Cause as exception, as that for which all else stands in. That is, he will reject the whole modern, Enlightenment idea of the Cause as sacrifice, as that which no object can adequately represent, for the postmodern, post-totalitarian idea of the Cause as the sacrifice of sacrifice, in which our ultimate fidelity to the Cause demands that it be given up.

When we look at what Žižek says about this Cause, we can see that it is always marked – and this is obviously indebted to Kant – by a certain 'as if' (*L*, 259). But, as opposed to the hypothetical nature of the Kantian 'as if', which refers to the regulative nature of Ideas, in Žižek this is meant to speak of the way that when we act motivated by the Cause we act 'as if' a particular state of affairs were *already* the case. And yet at the same time this is also to admit that things are *not* already this way; that, if we are able to act only because we know that things are already the way we say they are, they are also not like this until *after* we act. To put it another way, this 'as if' of Cause is simply the re-marking, the repetition, of reality: it does not to seek to change or add anything to what is there, but merely to register what already exists (*TS*, 129; *CHU*, 131). But to re-mark reality is already to open up a certain space in it, to provide another explanation for it; and it is just this space that is the space of Cause. We are always trying to speak of what makes what is possible, of what allows things to be as they are, of what has been excluded to ensure the world is as it is – and this is Cause itself.

To make all of this clearer, we look here at a number of Žižek's specific political decisions and commitments. To go back to what we said in Chapter 1 with regard to 'Why is Every Act?', even though every attempt to break out of the Symbolic only ends up repeating it, even though we only ever have the choice between two master-signifiers, the aim of the act, as Žižek says, is to 'maintain the fundamental choice' (*B*, 122), to pick the master-signifier that best stands in for what is excluded from the Symbolic.[1] Crucially, however – to return to Žižek's dispute with Kant and Derrida – this is not to defer the choice but can only be shown through it. It is only through some choice that we can think what cannot be chosen. And if all this still sounds vague or indeterminate, we take up in this chapter two of Žižek's actual political 'choices' in some detail. The first is his support of military force and even bombing by NATO during the 1990s Balkan wars. This, it must be recognized, is an interpretive *intervention* in the situation, because at the time he first began to urge this course of action, it was not yet part of official NATO policy. And Žižek backs up his argument there with very specific reasons, which he spells out at great length. But at the same time he also *criticizes* this military option, pointing out that it is not the best alternative, that it only stands in for what he really wants. The second example we look at is Žižek's response to the terrorist attacks on the World Trade Center of 11 September 2001, where again, while rejecting the temptation of terrorism, he also argues against the simple alternative between 'terrorism' and the 'war on terrorism'. That is, while always having to make a choice between alternatives, he is precisely guided in this by which of them best allows him to think what precedes this choice, what is excluded by this choice.

In this chapter, we pursue the consequences of this 'negation of negation' that characterizes the relationship between the master-signifier and the act. The master-signifier is neither the same as nor different from the act, but is revealed as the 'negation' of its 'negation', so that if there is nothing outside of the master-signifier it is nevertheless 'not-all'. And it is this feminine 'not-all' that has gradually emerged as the focus of Žižek's work, not just in the area of sexuality but also ethics, politics and even economics. (And it would be important to trace the development of Žižek's thinking on all of these issues, showing how it moves from a masculine 'exception' allowing a universality to a feminine 'not-all' from which there is no exception.) It is to imply, as we suggest, a completely different model of social action. It is no longer a matter of the realization of a transcendental possibility or of the potential becoming actual, but would be more directed by the idea that the transcendental is *already* empirical, the potential *already* actual – a 'quasi-transcendental' collapse of the distinction between level and metalevel that we have already seen on the feminine side of the 'formulae of sexuation' (*IR*, 157). But, again, this is not to be understood as a plea for indifference or for the doing away with of the distinction between the transcendental and the empirical. Rather, as Žižek says of Christianity, it is only on the basis that the Messiah has already arrived that we can be born again – or, as he puts it, 'for an authentic philosophy, everything has already happened; what is difficult to grasp is how this notion not only does not prevent engaged activity, but effectively sustains it' (*B*, 125). The world is at once all that is the case and – as opposed to any possibility of reconciliation, even in the far-off future – it can never entirely be realized, is always split by a kind of Cause or drive. And we attempt to sketch this logic of the 'not-all' or the 'negation of negation' here in three different realms, moving from where it is arguably first discovered to its most far-reaching consequences, from its most spiritual and unworldly to its most material and pragmatic: the feminine; Christianity and love; and politics and economics. In so doing, we might discern the outlines not so much of a 'Lacanian' politics, of which there has been some discussion recently, as of a 'feminine' or even a specifically 'Žižekian' ethics and politics.

Antigone and Medea

We have been using the expression 'not-all' here without properly explaining it. Although it was originally raised in the course of a discussion of Kant and Hegel, it first occurs in Žižek as an attempt to distinguish between the mathematical and dynamic sublimes in Kant (*TN*, 53–8). In fact, the notion of the 'not-all' ultimately derives from the feminine side of Lacan's 'formulae of sexuation'. On the masculine side of these formulae, we have a universality guaranteed by an exception. It is because one individual is not within the phallic order that all others are. Cultural examples of this include the so-called primal father, who is supposed to be able to enjoy all women directly, while all other men must operate within the limits of castration. However, we might think also of the Lady of courtly love or the *femme fatale* of film noir, for she too appears outside of the law of symbolic exchange, while all other women are inside it. On the feminine side of the formulae, by contrast, it is because there is nothing of woman outside of the symbolic order that she is not-all inside it. But this must be understood very carefully. Žižek in his elaboration of the formulae in *Indivisible Remainder* cautions us against two common misreadings of this feminine side. The first is again to understand some women (or woman as such) as outside of the symbolic order. This is perhaps as theorists such as Julia Kristeva and certain New Age feminists do when they speak of woman as 'unrepresentable'. As Žižek says, this is merely to repeat the basic male fantasy which wants to conceive of woman as not within the usual rules (*IR*, 159–60). The second, more subtle, misreading consists not in asserting some particular woman as outside of the symbolic order but some particular *part* of woman (*IR*, 156). Here, while not directly repeating the male fantasy, we replay it in a different way: while on the masculine side the split is external, on the feminine side it is *internal*. Through a kind of undetectable irony, woman adopts a distance on to the symbolic order. To come back to the Kantian analogy, what is proposed is a certain 'woman-in-herself', permanently beyond the reach of the masculine. There is always something beneath her surface appearance or veil, something that cannot be known about her, to take up for a moment the well-known notion of the 'feminine masquerade' (*IR*, 158).

It is interesting in this regard to consider Antigone, arguably the greatest figure of feminine ethics and politics. The classic psychoanalytic reading of Antigone's actions in opposing King Creon's refusal to allow her brother Polynices to be buried is undoubtedly Lacan's *Ethics*, which interprets them as pointing beyond an ethics of the 'Good' (*S7*, 240). Antigone clings to her decision to have him properly buried against the urgings of her family and friends, the King's warnings of the social unrest this will cause and perhaps even any 'objective' analysis of the situation. What this is taken to reveal by Lacan – and by Žižek following him – is that the authentic ethical act does not obey any pre-existing social consensus, does not conform to what is generally accepted as good, but itself defines what is good. It does not take place from within the existing symbolic order, but rather makes the symbolic order, brings about the conditions that would justify it. And Žižek speaks of this aspect of the act in terms that again allow him to criticize what he sees as the typical deconstructive strategy of deferral and passivity, its belief that any act can only ontologize and compromise the 'Other', which ultimately is only an excuse for putting off the act, not pursuing its consequences to the end. As he writes in *Totalitarianism?* of the performative 'equivalence' made between act and ground in Antigone:

> Does not Antigone stand for the exclusive and uncompromising attachment to the Other *qua* Thing, eclipsing the Other *qua* Third, the agency of mediation/ reconciliation? ... From the Lacanian perspective, this 'respect for Otherness' is the force of *resistance against the act*, against the 'crazy' short-circuit between the unconditioned and the conditioned, the ethical and the political (in Kantian terms: between the noumenal and the phenomenal), that 'is' the act. (*T?*, 158, 160)

But this passage must be read very carefully, for it represents by this stage in Žižek's work a certain shift in attitude towards Antigone. Although for much of his career Žižek had approved of Antigone, in the period immediately preceding *Totalitarianism?* he had opened up a certain distance on to her actions, arguing that with them we do not finally see that 'short-circuit' between the ground and the grounded, the conditioned and the unconditioned. That is, rather than a total identification with the act we have a separation from it. The act is grasped as an *exception*, as coming from a principle higher than the human (and it is important to note that, beyond the evocation of her brother, Antigone also speaks in the name of the gods). In other words, the totally successful or accomplished act continues to be understood as impossible, as a sign from another, transcendent, order of being. There is proposed again a Kantian emptiness, in which the 'Good' is seen as an abstract and finally unreachable principle, which cannot be attained in so far as we remain human. We would have the 'bad infinity' of the masculine dynamic sublime and not the 'good infinity' of the feminine mathematical sublime (*TN*, 55–7; *TS*, 166). It is the 'bad infinity', we might say, of the 'between two deaths', in so far as they are understood as different, in which we give up all (earthly) things for one (immortal) thing. As Žižek writes in the earlier *Fragile Absolute*:

> In the traditional (pre-modern) act, the subject sacrifices everything (all 'pathological' things) for the Cause–Thing that

matters to him more than life itself: Antigone, condemned to death, enumerates all the things she will *not* be able to experience because of her possible death (marriage, children ...) – this is the 'bad infinity' one sacrifices through the Exception (the Thing for which one acts, and which, precisely, is *not* sacrificed). Here the structure is that of the Kantian Sublime: the overwhelming infinity of the sacrificed empirical/pathological objects brings home in a negative way the enormous, incomprehensible dimension of the Thing for which one sacrifices them ... Is it necessary to add that *this* Antigone is a *masculine* fantasy *par excellence*? (*FA*, 154)

In other words – to go back to what we previously said about the various ways of misreading the feminine side of the 'formulae of sexuation' – we can see Antigone's 'unconditional' insistence on the Cause here not as something that reroutes the Symbolic but as what allows or entrenches it. We can understand her 'act' not as what breaks with the Symbolic but as that 'inherent transgression' necessary for it. For, in a sense, Antigone protests against the system only in the name of the system itself.[2] Exactly as Hegel criticizes Kant for the way his 'transcendental' is determined by what it would explain, so Antigone finally only accuses the system of not living up to its own standards. That is, she *holds back* the abstraction of the system by recalling it to a concrete exception and *holds out* a distance from the system (even if in its own name). And yet, as we have seen with the master-signifier, it is just this distance from the system that is the form of our most profound identification with it. As Žižek says in *Fragile Absolute*: 'The basic paradox of the relationship between public power and its inherent transgression is that the subject is actually "in" (caught in the web of) power only and precisely in so far as he does not fully identify with it' (*FA*, 148). And, to return to what we were saying about the misreading of the feminine side of the formulae of sexuation, the other way of understanding all this is that Antigone does what she does in the name of some specifically *feminine* moral position – as though woman were the guardian of 'universal' human values (*FA*, 155). But, again, this 'feminine' can be asserted only conservatively, only to preserve the system itself against its misrepresentation. That is, if Antigone sacrifices the possibility of marriage and children, she nevertheless does so only in the name of *family*. However, to this extent, she does not entirely identify with the Cause: just as she proposes a certain exception to Power, so there are certain things she will not give up in making her stand. As Žižek writes, contrasting

Antigone with that other great figure from Greek tragedy, Medea, who in the name of her children ends up sacrificing these very children:

> How are we to fight power? Through fidelity to the old organic Mores threatened by Power, or by out-violencing Power itself? Two versions of femininity: Antigone can still be read as standing for particular family roots against the universality of the public space of state Power; Medea, on the contrary, out-universalizes universal Power itself. (*B*, 158)

To make the comparison clearer, Antigone opposes Power in the name of something specific. She proposes an *exception to* (something left out from) the universality of Power. Medea is the opposite of this, in that she does not oppose something specific to Power, say it is too universal, but argues that its so-called universality is still too specific, in so far as it does have some exception. Antigone is prepared to sacrifice everything in the name of her Cause; Medea is prepared to sacrifice her Cause in the name of *nothing*. (And here there are two different ways of thinking exception: for Antigone, the exception is what is opposed to and allows universality; for Medea, the exception arises only as a retrospective effect of the *failure* of universality.) But, again, in order to try to think this, let us recall Žižek's outlining in *On Belief* of a series of progressively more complicated logics of sacrifice, each of which is aimed at producing or sustaining the fiction of a Big Other (*B*, 69–78). For this is what Antigone could be understood to be trying to convince us of by means of her sacrifice: that it precisely *is* a sacrifice, that there will be a 'Last Judgement' according to which she will be proved right. And it is just to this extent that Antigone does not totally identify with her Cause: it is fundamentally to prove that there is some underlying order or justice in the world that drives her on and not any justice for her brother. However, in *Totalitarianism?*, as part of his more recent 'positive' reading of Antigone, Žižek adds another twist to this in arguing that what Antigone might be said to reveal through her actions is that there is no Other, that this Other with whom we identify is only the 'abyss of freedom' in its terrifying openness. As he writes there of this 'other' Antigone:

> Again, in the act, in this moment of madness, the subject assumes the nonexistence of the Other-Thing – assumes, that is, the full burden of freedom *impervious* to any call of the Other. The act involves the acceptance of this double impossibility/limit: although our

empirical universe is incomplete, this does not mean that there is *another* 'true' reality that sustains it. (*T?*, 175)

But, again, this must be understood very carefully. It is not so much that Antigone's sacrifice is an attempt to cover up the lack of an Other, but that this sacrifice at once is only possible because there is no Other and can only lead to an Other. In other words, in this alternative reading of Antigone's actions, she does not appeal to pre-established values, does not contest the system in its own name, but knows there is no Other like this until *after* her sacrifice. In a manner similar to what we saw with Schelling, it is as though the system is already 'potentially' in place but does not actually exist until after Antigone's free sacrifice. That is, it is not our distance from the Other that undermines it, because this is only to imagine it as already existing, this can only end up producing an exception that allows it. Rather, it is only through our complete identi-fication with it that we might reveal it does not (yet) exist.

We might at this point turn to Medea and see in what ways she goes 'beyond' Antigone – or, at least, is closer to that paradoxical logic we are seeking to elaborate here. What is it that Žižek says about Medea in contrast to Antigone? The crucial aspect of Medea – and it is a 'striking against oneself' we find in a number of other important ethical exam-ples: *Ransom* (*CHU*, 122), *The Usual Suspects* (*CHU*, 122), *The Fight Club* (*L*, 252–3), Isabel Archer in *The Portrait of a Lady* (*B*, 78) and Julia Mot-tram in *Brideshead Revisited* (*B*, 149) – is that she kills the very children who are her Cause. She sacrifices the exception Antigone is seen to cling on to. Or, to put it in its most acute form, it is in order to save her Cause that she sacrifices her Cause. Her Cause is not caught up in any particu-lar object but is what goes beyond any particular object. And for Žižek this is not only the distinctively 'feminine' but also the peculiarly modern (we might even say postmodern) form of sacrifice. As he writes of Medea:

> In the modern ethical constellation, one *suspends this exception of the Thing* . . . In contrast to this ('masculine') universality of the struggle for power that relies on the ethical figure of Woman as its inherent exception, the ('feminine') ethical act proper involves the *suspension* of this exception. (*FA*, 154, 155)

It is a (post)modernity that is also to be seen in the Stalinist show trials, in which in the name of the Cause the defendants necessarily had to give up their own exceptionality, the acknowledgment by the Big Other that they were sacrificing themselves. (They were quite prepared to denounce themselves publicly so long as Stalin privately acknowledged their innocence, but it is precisely the 'greatness' of Stalin that he refused to do this [*T?*, 107–8].) In other words, there was no holding back for them from the ultimate sacrifice. To repeat what we said before, there was a necessarily complete identification by them with the Cause at the very moment that they realized that this Cause was empty or did not exist, at least without their own actions. And it is at this point that they were no longer 'between two deaths', for they were neither able to trade their mortal biological life for some immortal Cause nor to live on after their 'symbolic destitution' or abandonment by the Cause (*T?*, 96–7).[3]

But in all of this, what is meant by the fact that there is no Other? What is meant by saying that Medea goes 'beyond' the exception of Antigone and sacrifices even her Cause? In what sense does she 'out-violence' or 'out-universalize' Power? In her pure identification without reserve with the Cause, we want to suggest, what is opened up is not so much what is 'outside' or 'against' the Cause as what allows the Cause to be stated, that place from where it is spoken. (As opposed to Antigone, who is able to say that she is following some pre-existing Cause or is able to hold on to some exception outside of it, here we are precisely trying to put together the fact that there is no exception to the Cause, that we are totally caught up in it, and that it would not exist without us, that it is 'posited' or 'enunciated' by us.) It is not so much a matter of doing away with the Cause – as with the master-signifier or transference, we could break with any Cause only in the name of another Cause – as of that 'Cause' that underlies any Cause, that 'Cause' for which any Cause stands in. That is, even though the Cause always has to be named as a kind of exception, as what everything stands in for, it in turn only stands in for another, which allows it to be re-marked. This is ultimately what Žižek means by Medea 'out-violencing' and 'out-universalizing' Power: her showing that it is still too specific, still too much of an exception, still too much defined against what it resists. It is not to oppose the symbolic order, propose some other to it, but to reveal that it is *already* other, incomplete, only possible in so far as it stands in for an Other. It is not to 'transgress' it, but to act 'as if' it were *already* transgressed. We henceforth do 'what is allowed', but for entirely different reasons. It is an absolute identification that leads to an absolute difference (*FA*, 147–8; *T?*, 171–2). This is why with Medea Pure Good is indistinguishable from Diabolical Evil (false conformity or doing the right thing for the wrong reasons).[4] And, again, the decisive though difficult point to grasp is that, unlike Antigone, Medea does not do what she does in the name of another or higher law, because she does not stand outside of what is. This is the subtle difference between Antigone contesting the law in its own name (as though it can be stated as such outside of its own exception) and Medea showing that 'nothing' or drive underlying the law (the law from the beginning as only its own exception).

To put all this another way, we wonder whether it really is the giving up or sacrifice of the Cause that Žižek is wanting here. For this giving up is in the end impossible. The Cause can never entirely be given up because – exactly like the master-signifier – this giving up *is* what the Cause is. This is the final distinction to be made between Antigone and Medea: just as the Cause always hints at something beyond it that it is the betrayal of – this is the Kantian/hysterical aspect of Antigone, in which her refusal to compromise is secretly driven by the fear that nothing could truly satisfy her – so Medea for her part must keep on repeating her sacrifice because the Cause keeps on returning. And this, again, is the real meaning of Cause as introducing a kind of 'not-all' in the perpetual folding over of something (the exception) on to itself. We cannot have any kind of a finitude or immanence (non-Cause) without it being re-marked (by a Cause). As Alenka Zupančič writes in her essay in the Žižek-edited collection *Sexuation*: 'It is the exception which becomes immanent to the all of the finite and thus introduces an opening in this finitude, making it infinite' (*S*, 289). That is, the 'infinitude' of Cause is not simply some other space but precisely what means that the phenomenal is all that is the case, that the phenomenal is 'infinite'. It is the Cause as what renders what is 'not-all' that also allows it to be 'all', to be its own Cause. In a sense, it is the logic of the re-mark, but the logic of the re-mark applied to itself infinitely. It is thus not ultimately a matter of opposing Hegel to Kant or Medea to Antigone. Rather, Hegel and Medea are perhaps that 'not-all' that allows Kant and Antigone to become 'all'. They are those 'vanishing mediators' that mean that henceforth we can only think in terms of Kant, Antigone and the masculine exception.

We see all this in undoubtedly the two greatest examples of this feminine ethics in cinema: King Vidor's *Stella Dallas* and Lars von Trier's *Breaking the Waves*. The first is the story of a lower-class woman, Stella Dallas (played by Barbara Stanwyck), who marries an upper-class man, only to become disillusioned with and estranged from him. She divorces him to allow him to get back with his first love, the woman with whom he was forced to break up when his father became bankrupt, while she retreats from the world with her daughter Laurel. But in the end Stella gives up Laurel, so that she too can enter into the same

upper-class marriage that had proved so disappointing to her. Nevertheless, in the famous last shot of the film, after Stella has lost everything and
been forsaken by her daughter, she steps with a radiant glow on her face
out of the camera's range and into a new and uncertain world. And the
profound enigma the film poses is: why? Why is Stella so happy at this
point when she should be at her lowest? We follow in our attempt to
answer this question the extraordinary reading of *Stella Dallas* by Joan
Copjec in her essay 'More! From Melodrama to Magnitude'. She
begins by making the point that in the usual interpretations of the film
Stella is seen as a kind of *hysteric*. Like Antigone, she would reject the 'all'
of the world by clinging to the Cause of her daughter, for whom she seeks
to make an advantageous match. She would sacrifice everything – as we
saw earlier with those logics of sacrifice – to prove that there is a Big
Other, an underlying order to the world (that her original belief in marriage was not mistaken, despite her own unhappy experience of it).
Indeed, Copjec pushes this argument further than most in suggesting
that Stella even tries to get her own estranged husband back with the
woman he had intended to marry in order to keep alive this illusion of
phallic power and potency ('MM', 263). That is, like any good hysteric,
Stella organizes her own romantic failure (for example, giving up the
sympathetic and goodnatured Ed Munn), so that her beliefs do not actually have to be tested. She takes more pleasure in complaining about
society than in any direct fulfilment in it.

However, against this reading – which remains fundamentally masculine, with its idea of an 'exception' allowing a universal order –
Copjec argues that in the last shot of the film we must understand Stella
not as running *away* from the world, setting herself apart from it, but as
rejoining the world, becoming part of it again. She no longer wants to be
morally 'superior', different from others, but anonymous, submerged in
the crowd. And it is this, Copjec provocatively argues, that is the cause of
what we might call the non-phallic *jouissance*, the particular feminine
pleasure, the slow-spreading smile, that seems to course through her
body at this point. It is to begin to think – to take us back to that 'psychotic' point outside of the symbolic order we saw in 'Why is Every
Act?' – the way that Stella at once is never more under the phallic rule,
judged as a failure as both mother and wife, and has never been more
free, more able to decide (to repeat her decision) whether to join the
symbolic order or not. As Copjec writes:

What is voiced is something like a command or a kind of carnal cry:
'More!' This cry does not mark some lack of coincidence between

the Symbolic and the Real, but their fleshy/formal join. Yet the
cry is not a statement, it does not describe the absolute all, a universe
without exception; it is an imperative to speak. It enjoins us to
say all, to speak of every singularity, without exception.
('MM', 269–70)

As Copjec suggests, with this collapse of the distinction between the
Symbolic and the Real, Stella is perhaps not so much a hysteric as *psycho-tic*. There is a kind of equivalence made between the Symbolic and
the Real, in much the same way as a psychotic literally hears voices in
their head – but not quite. Copjec does not in fact speak of the direct
coincidence or equivalence of the two, but of their 'fleshy/formal join'.
It would be to speak of the final *impossibility* of making them equivalent,
of the way the Symbolic is all but only because of the Real. But it is also to
speak of the infinite task of trying to think this Real, of incessantly fold-ing any supposed universal over on to itself to show that it is always only
particular. To put this another way, what Copjec speaks of here is not so
much anything enunciated as enunciation itself, the necessity simply to
keep on speaking. And, strangely enough, the other word Copjec uses
to describe this is 'love', which is what Lacan famously defines as 'giving
what one does not have' ('MM', 269). And this might be another way of
thinking Stella's relationship to so-called hysterical sacrifice: that what
is sacrificed is only an after-effect of it being sacrificed; that the symbolic
order in which things have value only arises after a 'free' sacrifice for no
end. It is perhaps finally not a matter of Stella refusing sacrifice – she is
not psychotic – but rather of her knowing that what she sacrifices exists
only as lost, which is also to say that this symbolic order does not exist
without her.[5]

We see this connection between psychosis and feminine *jouissance* also
in *Breaking the Waves*. The film tells the story of a naïve, simple-minded
young woman, Bess (played by Emily Watson), who marries a rig-worker, Jan, who ends up crippled by an industrial accident. In the ter-rible climax to the film, Bess, who believes she is able to cure Jan by
engaging in sex acts with strangers, sails off to a ship where she has pre-viously been beaten, knowing in advance the fate that awaits her. The
extraordinary aspect of this is that by this point Jan has already aban-doned her, signing the papers that would commit her to an asylum. She
nevertheless goes ahead; and, in the final scene of the film, we discover
that Jan has indeed been cured. The now-dead Bess is then signalled by
an impossible aerial shot of church bells ringing out from the sky, which
goes against the rules of the strict religious community in which she

lived, where they were banned. Again here, it is tempting to say that Bess is either a *hysteric*, in so far as she sacrifices herself to keep up the myth of male potency (she performs sex acts in order that she can tell her husband, as though he could commit them himself), or *psychotic*, in so far as she believes that she is in direct contact with a God who can organize miracles (she does in fact speak to Him throughout the film). However, as with *Stella Dallas*, the absolutely decisive aspect of *Breaking the Waves* is that Bess still carries on with her sacrifice after Jan/God has abandoned her. It is precisely only her free act of faith, from which she does not except herself (she dies without witnessing Jan's cure), that leads to a miracle. And, again, the enigmatic fact is that it is just at this moment of her final destiny, when, like Antigone walking towards that grave in which she will be buried, she sails in a boat towards the ship in which she will die, that a beautiful smile crosses her face – the very image of feminine *jouissance*. At once she is completely outcast, shunned by her community and abandoned by her husband, and at her most unconstrained, entirely undetermined by any symbolic rule. Or, as Žižek says in his essay on the film, 'Death and the Maiden', Bess does not so much 'suffer for the Other as enjoy for him' (*ZR*, 214). Like Bernini's sculpture of St Teresa, as analysed by Lacan, her smile is that of a saint who has no need of an Other in 'becoming her own Cause' (*AF*, 85), because she knows she is the only proof necessary of God's existence.

Judaism and Christianity

Copjec speaks of love in her essay on *Stella Dallas* as the imperative to say 'all', to speak of 'every singularity, without exception'. This appears at first contradictory or counter-intuitive. We tend to think of love – for example, the love of our fellow human beings – as universal, as refusing to make exceptions. Žižek, however, disagrees. For him, the crucial aspect of love – or, at least, of Christian love, which is the version he argues for – is that it *is* so partial, so specific. It does not love everybody equally, but always introduces finer and finer distinctions. But on what basis exactly does it do this? It does not love the other simply for their individuality or idiosyncrasy (for their difference from us) (*FA*, 125), but rather for what takes them beyond themselves (for their difference from themselves) (*L*, 214–15). And what this forces us to think – along the lines of Copjec's injunction always to speak more singularly, to exclude no exception – is that what is at stake here is a specificity that goes beyond any symbolic identity, a certain 'symptom' or 'tic' that keeps on dividing the person it inhabits. It is only in this way – by taking into account that 'particular absolute' that means there is no whole – that love can become universal. This is the real 'universality' of Christianity, as opposed to, say, Judaism (*TS*, 226). It is why Christianity is more specific than Judaism (it is not just a matter of some 'Chosen People' or following a set of external rituals, but of a kind of inner belief, which we are always falling short of); but it is also why it is more universal (*anyone* can be touched by God's grace, *anyone* can be converted or 'born again'). It is also the 'universality' of the proletariat, as opposed to the working class (*TS*, 227). The notion of the working class remains too objective, ontological, in a way too exclusive, as opposed to that of the proletariat, which at once is no longer a matter of objective economic identification but something anyone can belong to (intellectuals, the unemployed, immigrants) and exists nowhere in reality, cannot be empirically defined.

But, to begin with, it needs to be realized that Žižek *approves of* many aspects of Judaism. It is a worldly, practical religion (hence the stereotypical anti-Semitic cliché of a Jewish person who is able to reconcile their mercantile activities with their religious beliefs). Its rules are clearly stated in the Torah, and it is only a matter of following them to be Jewish. As with the form of politics Žižek argues for – an organized politics along Party lines – with Judaism it is not so much a matter of our beliefs as our *actions*: 'Jews do not have to *declare* their belief, they immediately show it in their practice' (*B*, 129). There is a kind of 'immanence' in Judaism, a refusal of the 'otherworldly', that he likes. Indeed, at first sight Christianity can only appear *less* like what Žižek is arguing for. It is, after all, the religion *par excellence* of guilt and double-meaning, of endless interpretation and the tracking down of sin. It is the religion of 'inherent transgression', in which we are always racked with guilt for not properly following the law or following it for the wrong reasons (*TS*, 148–51). As opposed to the literality and finally non-authoritarian nature of Judaism – whose rules are openly stated for all to understand – there are the incessant doctrinal disputes and schisms that characterize the history of Christianity, the need for a complex hierarchy to mediate our relationship to God. And yet, despite this, Žižek continues to insist that it is Christianity that offers us a practical model for politics, that it is Christianity that finally breaks with the superegoic Other (guilt and bad conscience). How is this so? How is it that it is Christianity and not Judaism that goes furthest in thinking the non-existence of the Big Other? How is it that it is Christianity that better avoids that 'inherent transgression' that continues to bind us to power?

The answer to these questions is to be found in the Jewish necessity for *iconoclasm*, the prohibition of images of God. For it is to suggest that, even though everything can be made clear in Judaism, even though there is no obvious superego, there is nevertheless one exception, one thing that must be denied: the very founding of the law itself (*B*, 137). And Žižek goes further than this in claiming that – as with the Freudian theory of prohibition, which converts what is impossible into something that seems possible – Judaism's banning of images of God precisely gives the impression that there *is* some God beyond His image, something that *should not* be represented (*B*, 130–32). In other words – and here the analogy with a kind of masculine logic should be clear – the 'universality' of Judaism, the fact that it requires no Other, is possible only because of a certain exception, because there is one thing that cannot be spoken of (the founding of the law). As Žižek writes in *On Belief*, which contains his most detailed explication of the differences between Christianity and Judaism: 'Judaism is a religion whose public discourse is haunted by the spectral shadow of its obscene uncanny double, of its excessive transgressive founding violent gesture' (*B*, 137). Nevertheless, despite this, Christianity can only continue to strike us as a religion of guilt and bad conscience. In it, meaning is always doubled, nothing is what it seems. However, if its law is ultimately unknowable, this is not because it is *outside* of us (as is, if not the law, at least the origins of the law in Judaism), but because it is *inside* us, because we are responsible for it – this is the 'transcendental' nature of the Kantian moral subject, as brought out by Hegel (*IR*, 169; *PF*, 221–2; *TS*, 365–6). But this is also to say that, even though in the Christian religion there is no place to hide, even though we always fall short of the law, disobey it even in following it, we are also absolutely free, entirely undetermined, at every moment 'born again', in so far as it is posited *by us*. Or, to put this in Žižek's slightly abbreviated terms, the actual content of Christianity is in the end like Judaism, except that it is narrated *by us*. As he says: 'As to the content of the belief, one should be a Jew, while retaining the Christian position of enunciation' (*B*, 141). But, again – to go back to the connection between the 'all' and the 'not-all' – it is crucial to realize that this enunciation is not simply some exception that cannot be spoken of, as in the Jewish prohibition, but a kind of permanent *doubling* that at once means we can never entirely say what Christianity is and we are always being judged according to it.

Žižek will often describe this Christian overcoming of the distinction between law and sin – we might even say between enunciated and enunciation – in terms of a 'New Beginning', a 'wiping of the slate clean' (*TS*, 153; *B*, 144). But it is important to know exactly what this means.

It does not mean that we can forever avoid any symbolic accounting, that we can indefinitely put off our debts, that suddenly everything is rendered null and void. In the first instance, it means that that the grounds for our actions do not pre-exist us but are begun again each time we act, only arise as a result of their free positing by the subject. In order to begin to explain this, let us look at the difference between the Jewish and the Christian conceptions of the 'split' between act and belief. Žižek in *On Belief* quotes the famous Jesuit maxim: 'Here, then, is the first rule of acting: assume/believe that the success of your undertakings depends entirely on you, and in no way on God; but, nonetheless, set to work as if God alone will do everything, and you yourself nothing' (*B*, 125). He then cautions that this must be distinguished from the similar-looking (and usual): 'Believe that God guides your hand, but act as if everything depends on you' (*B*, 126). What is the difference? In the latter, even though it appears to be a matter of relying on ourselves, there is a kind of fetishistic 'split' in which we still secretly rely on the Other: we pretend to try, but we know that in the end everything is out of our hands. Indeed, this attitude might even be compared to Antigone's, who did not entirely commit herself to the act because she believed she spoke in the name of the Good. And we see this even in Judaism, despite its seeming to do away with the Big Other: for all of its emphasis on our beliefs lying in our acts, it still supposes that this symbolic order already exists and is merely played out by us. It does not pose the question – as we have seen, it is just this it prohibits – of *how* the symbolic order actually comes into being. In Christianity, by contrast – and this, again, is how we might understand Žižek's statement that with regard to the substance of our beliefs we should be Jewish, but with regard to the position of their enunciation we should be Christian – if it rejects the fetishistic split between acts and beliefs, which ends up denying the reality of our acts, it is not simply a matter of our acts but also of our beliefs. Why still this question of belief? We might say that this Christian attitude is an *inversion* of the usual fetishistic split: there belief is understood as an exception to or a miraculous suspension of Cause (hence the way we speak of the suspension of *disbelief*). We think we start with the act but we always end up with belief. On the contrary, with Christianity – and we might see the connection here with a similar inversion performed by Schelling (*IR*, 16) – we start with belief and end up with act. It is not a question of how our belief intervenes in an already existing field of acts, but of how acts themselves are not possible outside a certain belief. There are only acts, but this only because of belief – a belief that is not an exception to these acts, but precisely what renders them 'not-all'.

It is this argument for the 'subjective' imperfection of the objective, the 'subjectivizing' of substance, that is the profoundly Hegelian lesson of Žižek's work (*B*, 146; *L*, 179–80). Undoubtedly, it is tempting to understand this 'subject' as a kind of exception for which all else stands in, as in something like the endless metonymy of *desire*. However, as Žižek's work develops, he seeks to rewrite this 'limit' in terms of *drive* (*TN*, 128–30). To pull the threads of our argument together, we move perhaps from a world organized by the *master-signifier* (a universality guaranteed by an exception) to a world organized by the *symptom* or '*sinthome*' (not an exception but what introduces a split into what is). It is not so much a matter of an exception as of a certain 'nothing' that allows the exception (the master-signifier) to be named (*TS*, 108; *B*, 93). This, again, is the lesson of Christianity as opposed to Judaism in its assertion of the 'coincidence, identity even, between the sublime [God in the form of Christ] and the everyday object [the human]' (*B*, 92). God in Christianity is not simply a 'transcendental' exception, something above the human for which it stands in, reducing earthly life to a kind of shadow or endless waiting. Rather, in Christianity the catastrophe has already happened; God has already come back to earth (*B*, 126). And this is to say that God – like all true universals, all true Causes – is not some prohibited exception or what cannot be represented. He is not what introduces a split between this world and somewhere else. He is instead what introduces a split between this world *and itself*, between the human *and itself*. As Žižek says in *On Belief* (and this is strictly analogous to the way that in 'concrete universality' the universal is just what stops the particular being particular, the universal itself is only one of its particulars):

> Christ is fully a man only in so far as He takes upon Himself the excess/remainder, the 'too much' on account of which a man, precisely, is never fully a man: his Formula is not Man = God, but man = man, where the divine dimension intervenes only as that 'something' which prevents man from attaining his full identity. (*B*, 131–2)

And, to return to the notion of the 'negation of negation', it is not as though man is supplemented by Christ here, as though there is some secret dimension beyond things – this is the Kantian sublime Hegel rejects. Rather, this 'failure' just *is* things themselves: at once this other dimension is not what comes before but can only be seen through the 'failure' of things (just as the Real does not exist outside of the Symbolic but is only to be seen as a certain limitation arising within it) and things are always their own 'failure' (because of the Real). Like that 'fetish' of the Jew we looked at earlier (*SO*, 126), but generalized, everything is both itself and its own failure, only what is and something else. This other space is nothing but what Žižek calls the space of the world's *reduplicatio* or inscription: the grimace (*B*, 80), the smile (*B*, 98), the fleeting act of kindness (*L*, 202) ... We might say precisely the faces of those women at the end of our melodramas.

It is at this point that we come back to perhaps the most complicated matter of all in this comparison between Judaism and Christianity. As we say, in an obvious sense, Judaism with its explicit stating of the laws, its circumventing (perhaps proscribing) of interpretation, appears much closer to that state Žižek wants where there is no Other. It is, indeed, close to that moment at the end of the treatment when the analyst's words can be taken directly without any attempt to see them another way (*FA*, 139–40). But, in fact, Žižek insists that it is only Christianity that is able to go beyond this dialectic between the law and sin, that is able to do away with the problem of there always being another meaning behind the obvious one. So the question is: how is Christianity, with its incessant interpretation, its 'New Beginnings', able to become this indifferent drive, this simple doing of 'what is allowed' (*FA*, 147)? How is this possible when all is exception, all is 'sinthome' (*FA*, 115–16; *T?*, 100). And the answer is: *because in this doing of 'what is allowed' it is undecidable whether this is to follow or to produce a symbolic order. It is undecidable whether the act follows a prior guarantee or this guarantee arises only after the act.* It is this that Žižek means when he speaks of the act somehow going 'beyond' interpretation (as in the case of a woman who because of her religious convictions refuses a blood transfusion, even at the cost of her life (*FA*, 137–41)). It is not that it is uninterpretable – we are always able to show that it is said for the 'wrong' reasons – but that we cannot know *how* it will be interpreted. This is not that fetishistic split between knowing and believing, of not wanting to concern ourselves with the symbolic consequences of our actions, but rather arises because (we know that) the symbolic order does not exist until *after* we have contracted with it. In a sense, that is, Žižek is able to reconcile here Jewish literalism (the enunciated law) and the Christian taking into account of the prohibited remainder (its place of enunciation). It is not, however, to think this other place as an *exception* (the Jewish response), but *what is* as already its own exception. *Every* aspect of the symbolic order hints at – or, better, *is* – that place outside of it from where it comes about.

How are we to conceptualize this? In Christianity, there is no other to the law, to what is. And yet at the same time an impossible 'Other Space'

(*FA*, 158) is opened up that can no longer be seen as a fantasmatic supplement to social reality (as it still is in Judaism). Žižek speaks of this as
though it is finally to break with the masculine logic of exception, or
as though it is to reveal that this masculine logic arises in response to a
prior logic of the feminine (*B*, 97); but this is too simple. In fact, there is
only ever the exception – as the Cause is only ever a master-signifier.
The only difference is that on the Christian/feminine side this Jewish/
masculine exception is taken to its limit, in an attempt always to find
that enunciation behind any enunciated. It is *this* that is drive and the
Christian 'New Beginning': not the final sublation of difference but the
perpetual striving towards it. It is precisely the attempt, within the Symbolic, to make enunciation equal the enunciated, to repeat that 'forced
choice' before the 'fall of the binary signifier'. That is, this act is itself
repetition and its status as an act lies only in its repetition. And this is
why Žižek can say that Christian love, with its simultaneous coupling
and uncoupling, is hard work, why it does not occur just once or sponta-
neously but is proved only in its very duration and commitment (*FA*,
129). Again, if Christian drive proceeds on the basis that things are
already the way it says they are, its aim is also to make them like this.
Drive can never come to an end – as we spoke previously of our ethical
heroes going on forever – not because there is some external limit to be
overcome but because the very thing that allows it to make its equivalence always remains, persists as a kind of 'exception'. And it is *this*
gap – not of a void to be filled in, but of a certain simultaneity – that is
the 'gap' of drive, a 'gap' that it at once seeks to overcome and perpetu-
ates (*B*, 95–7).

It is in this sense, finally, that Žižek speaks of Christian love: as a certain 'nothing' that means that what is is 'not-all'. As he writes in *Fragile
Absolute*: 'Love is not an exception to the All of knowledge, but precisely
that "nothing" which makes even the complete series/field of knowledge
incomplete' (*FA*, 146). That is, to repeat what we have just said about
drive, if love is always looking for or working for love, so this working for love is already love. (And it is in this sense, incidentally, that
Žižek can say that striving for freedom *is* freedom [*TN*, 158] and seeking
happiness is already happiness [*L*, 260].) Something like this can be
seen – again, the equivalence between the act and repetition – in the
way the revolutionaries of Russia almost immediately re-enacted the
storming of the Winter Palace after its successful capture (*L*, 260). Not
only is there raised here the question of the way the Revolution was from
the beginning conceived of as the repetition of another – the French of
the Roman, the Russian of the French – but also of why the Revolution

must be constantly repeated, does not exist until after it has been repeated. This is the connection Žižek makes between the 'as if' and the notion of Revolution: it is at once to understand Revolution as if it has already happened and as 'not yet' a Revolution, an 'as if' Revolution. And it is this simultaneous equivalence and inequivalence that is the logic not of desire but of *drive*. As opposed to the simple deferral of desire, in which no object is able to satisfy us and we are always moving on to the next, producing a kind of repetition, it is only the 'equivalence' of drive that, though a kind of repetition, is able to produce something new. We come back to the long-running Hegelian theme in Žižek that it is the very attempt to look for the missing object that brings it about, that we would not be looking for it unless it had already been found (*SO*, 160–61; *TK*, 170–71). It is not so much that we simply have what we are looking for, but that we realize we already had it, that our current state of affairs cannot be explained except because of it (*SO*, 217–18; *TK*, 165–6; *TN*, 147–50). This again is what we mean by 'as if': it is at once a certain projection, disavowal, suspension of disbelief and only doing 'what is allowed'. The act is not so much impossible/deferred as at once only the following out of what already is and never able to be finished. And this is why, to conclude, the way the world actually is is not to be opposed to the endless doubling of drive but is inseparable from it. For if the doubling of drive can only take us back to where we started (if every act is only a repetition), where we start each time is also necessarily incomplete, different, possible only because of this repetition (every repetition is an act). As with Schelling's 'formula of the world', there is at once a constant 'raising to a higher power' as we try to speak of what is left out at each turn and we always return to where we began.

A politics of the 'not-all'

This 'utopianism' can also take a more directly 'political' form in Žižek's work. But this does not mean that it simply 'actualizes' itself, or passes over to 'reality'. Its aim is not immediately to be implemented. It is undoubtedly for this reason that commentators frequently complain of the 'impracticality' of Žižek's specific political proposals. For example, Laclau in one of his responses in *Contingency, Hegemony, Universality* writes: 'Žižek asserts that the proponents of postmodernism "leave out of sight the resignation at its heart, the acceptance of capitalism as 'the only game in town'" ... The difficulty with assertions like this is that they mean absolutely nothing' (*CHU*, 205–6). Or Robert S. Boynton, in his article 'Enjoy Your Žižek!' in *Lingua Franca*, writes: 'As philosophy,

Žižek's argument is breath-taking, but as a social prescription "dream" may be an apt word.' [6] And, indeed, Žižek himself will even repeat this kind of argument with regard to other theorists' work. For example, he will criticize Michael Hardt and Antonio Negri's *Empire* for its 'formal emptiness and impossible radicalization' (*L*, 331). But all of this is not to understand the essential task of philosophy, not to grasp its particular powers and properties. It is not to see its essential *abstraction* – Žižek amusingly cites Jameson to the effect that philosophy concerns not so much Italy as the *idea* of Italy (*TN*, 2). And it is not see its special form of *actuality* – the refusal of all post-Enlightenment philosophies to derive their ideas from any transcendent 'universality' (*AF*, 28).[7] However, to take all this up in more detail, let us look at just one of Žižek's suggestions: to 'cut off the head' of a company like Microsoft and make it freely available to all who want it, or to think that there is no need to do so because it is *already* socialized (*TS*, 350; *L*, 293). Now, in one sense, this is obviously untrue: a company like Microsoft is the very embodiment of today's 'frictionless capitalism' (*L*, 278). And yet, in another sense – to return to Žižek's point about the positive order being only the 'normalization' of an earlier negation – we *can* see Microsoft as based on or repressing a prior socialization (both Bill Gates' early career as a hacker and the continual hacking of Microsoft).

Along these lines, Žižek at a certain point in his work alludes to the famous Thesis 11 from Marx's *Theses on Feuerbach*: 'Philosophers have hitherto only interpreted the world; the point is to change it.' But he reverses it: for him, to think about the world *is* to change it (*PF*, 90–91). However, what is this to say? What does it mean to suggest that thought is part of reality? Žižek in *Ticklish Subject* looks at Kant's well-known response to the 'enthusiasm' that greeted the French Revolution (*TS*, 139–40). The way it is usually read is that the conservative Kant approved of this sublime emotion, but not of what it stood for; that he made impossible any actual social change in warning against the too-close identification with the object of this emotion. But Kant's real point is that this 'enthusiasm', even if misdirected, is a form of freedom; that, beyond any object it is felt for, the very fact of this 'enthusiasm' is a kind of revolution. And *this* is the power of thought, so close to the equivalence between enunciated and enunciation, that is played on throughout Žižek's work. It is in this sense that thinking is a force, testifies to freedom, is freedom itself embodied. It is in this sense that Žižek is able to say that thinking makes itself true. And *this* is what it means to say that to think Microsoft is socialized *is* that it is socialized. It is this freedom to think that *is* this socialization, just as it *is* the ultimate success of the French Revolution. And *this* is what Hegel's critique of Kant's notion of freedom as 'transcendental' seeks to bring out: not only that 'freedom' is more 'transcendental' than Kant says, in so far as he can only characterize it in terms of this world, but also that it is not 'transcendental' at all, in so far as it is evidenced in Kant's very thinking of it. That is, Hegel does not aim to surpass Kant but to show that he has already found the solutions to his problems, not so much in anything he actually says as in his saying of it (*TS*, 60–61, 84–6).

Again, however, all this must be understood very carefully. The ultimate point of Hegel's demonstration that freedom is not transcendental is that it is neither unrealizable (as with Kant) nor merely equivalent to its realization (as with Badiou). Rather, freedom at once exists here and now *and* can never be realized. First of all, as we have seen, working for, writing of, thinking about freedom *is* freedom. Freedom exists not elsewhere, but is to be seized at every moment. This is what Žižek emphasizes in his account of Lenin and his break with the Mensheviks on the eve of the Russian Revolution: that it was not a question of waiting until the 'objective' conditions were right before deciding to act (*T?*, 114–17; *B*, 84). Rather, Lenin's conception of the situation as 'exceptional' – and as always being 'exceptional' – meant that he did not have to wait for the circumstances that would justify his actions, but that he could act *now*. Paradoxically, it was Lenin's conception of the circumstances as 'exceptional' that meant he could entirely occupy his own time, that there was no other moment than the present. It is for this reason too that Žižek (following Brecht and Lenin) can approve of Conservatives more than most self-marginalizing Leftists: at least they are actually prepared to assume power, make the difficult decisions, in order to achieve their aims. It is why he can even go on to support Lenin's eventual depoliticization of the Revolution, his handing of it over to scientists and bureaucrats (*L*, 272). It is indeed what he likes about Lacan (and St Paul) in suggesting that the truth of psychoanalysis is to be found as much in his organizational papers as in his Seminars. That is, Žižek precisely uses the language of *Party* throughout his work: in *Revolution at the Gates*, for example, he will speak of 'psychoanalytic associations' and 'subversive half-illegal political organizations' (*L*, 309). The Party *formalizes* the Revolution in the sense that it institutionalizes it, gives it structure, breaks with the ideology of 'spontaneism' and 'popular sentiment' (*L*, 187). And 'terrorism' for Žižek is just this refusal to go all the (political) way: to avoid the necessity for Party organization, which is not at all a compromise but is the only form a true global revolution, any actual alternative to capitalism, can take (*L*, 270).

But at the same time as this 'immanence', there is also something else to be seen. It is to think that, despite the emphasis on the actual practice of Lenin, his institutionalization of Marx, there is nevertheless a certain 'Lenin' beyond any such 'Leninism', or a Lenin 'beyond' Stalin. That is, if the destiny of Marxism is to be institutionalized, it is also to be what would render this forever incomplete. If Marxism is absolutely self-defining, in the present, it is also open at every point, a philosophy in which miracles *do* happen: as with Lenin at the advent of the Revolution, it is never entirely a matter of 'objective' circumstances, but always of a certain leap into the unknown. It is this that ultimately condemns Stalinism and contemporary 'Third Way' politics, both of which are a kind of 'perversion', in which power is pursued for its own sake. Indeed, we might even restate this relationship between the transcendent and the immanent, the act and the Symbolic, in terms of the relationship between politics and economics: if politics needs economics with its procedures of realization and actualization, economics for its part needs politics, which is a way of thinking that which cannot be planned or accounted for (that is, the imperfection or nonexistence of the Big Other). The relationship between politics and economics, as Žižek says in a striking metaphor, is like the famous optical illusion of 'two faces or a vase' (*L*, 271). Each totalizes the field without exception, leaving us nothing else to see; but only because of the other. Each means that the other is 'not-all'. To put it another way, this formalization of politics (or of economics) is a kind of *drive*: at the same moment as it entirely accounts for itself (is its own sublation), it always has more to do. This is why it is always a matter of 'repeating' Lenin (*L*, 11, 310). We repeat something only in so far as it is unfinished, in so far as it has not yet happened.

We can see this 'not-all', for instance, in a number of statements that Žižek makes about capitalism. Following Deleuze and Guattari's *Anti-Oedipus*, Žižek begins with Marx's great statement from the *Grundrisse* that the only limit to capitalism is capitalism itself (*TS*, 358; *FA*, 17; *L*, 274–5). This can be understood, in just that way we have tried to outline, as saying that, as opposed to any 'masculine' notion of a simple exception to capitalism (revolution, catastrophic breakdown or collapse), there is a kind of 'feminine' not-all at stake in it (there is at once no limit to capitalism and capitalism is its own limit). But this must be interpreted very deliberately. In a sense – as with the various misreadings of the feminine side of the 'formulae of sexuation' – it is tempting to think of this as though there is still some actual outside to capitalism, some real limit to it. In fact, against this, the very consequence of this limit is that there is no limit, no outside to capitalism. And, as Žižek says, this means both that all critiques of capitalism are only 'reformist' and that capitalism turns all crises into new opportunities for investment (*L*, 277). It is therefore not a matter, as Deleuze and Guattari already made clear, of criticizing capitalism from any 'negative' position. And yet this also means that we cannot, as many commentators, including Marx, once believed, have the dynamics of capitalism without this limit (*TN*, 209–10; *FA*, 17–18; *B*, 18–19; *L*, 274–5). And this is to say that if there is no outside or limit to capitalism, no objective breakdown or collapse, capitalism is also nothing, has no inside; the breakdown has already occurred. To take us back to what we previously said with regard to 'concrete universality', it is not only a question of the 'universality' of capitalism but of that even wider 'universality' – let us call it class struggle – of which capitalism is only a part, and which renders it 'not-all' (*L*, 267–8). This is why – and this is undoubtedly his most complicated gesture of all here – Žižek is able to say that even if there is no foreseeable alternative to capitalism, the catastrophe will still happen. For Žižek, the true utopians are not those who believe the end of capitalism will happen, but those who believe it will not happen (that is, that it has not already happened) (*CHU*, 324).

It is something like this that explains that 'undecidability' we find in Žižek's actual political decisions. As we have tried to show, it has always been a matter of a certain 'split' opened up by authentic thought. And it is this splitting of what is, the revealing of that antagonism that underlies our necessarily forced choice, that is the real way thought operates in political discourse, as opposed to any common-sense idea of proposing some political programme stable in advance. It is the idea, taken from Kantian ethics, that we are always wrong in advance, that every choice is incorrect. It is the idea, taken from Lacan's work on psychosis, that there is always a 'worse' that precedes the 'bad' of the forced choice that is somehow 'better' (*TS*, 377). But, in order to analyse this in greater detail, let us look at two of Žižek's recent political interventions: the first concerning the NATO bombing of Kosovo during the 1990s Balkan wars; and the second the 11 September terrorist attacks on the World Trade Center. They have both raised strong responses to their 'opinions'; but the truly radical thing about them – this is, in fact, what most people were responding to, whether they knew it or not – is that they propose no 'solutions', that they avoid the temptation to take sides. Or, more precisely, it is that all present solutions, both sides of the conflict, are shown to be 'bad', not the best possible outcome. That is, with regard to the NATO 'peace-keeping' mission in the Balkans, Žižek is not against the military option as such. As he says: 'I rather think that it is the pacifist position – "More bombs and killing never bring peace" – which is a fake, and that one should heroically endorse the paradox of a militaristic pacifism' (*FA*, 57). However, he also questions this alternative, not only for its obvious selectivity and ties to Western strategic interests but also for the way it takes place in the name of some 'depoliticized universal human rights' (*FA*, 57), which effectively disempowers the very people it claims to be helping. With regard to the terrorist strikes of 11 September, Žižek condemns the simple passage to the act of the hijackers, with their desire for some 'spectacular effect of the Real' (*DR!*, 10) and their 'morbid culture of death, the attitude which finds the climactic fulfilment of one's life in violent death' (*DR!*, 141). But he also condemns the American fantasy that it is somehow immune from the effects of its actions (*DR!*, 17–19, 26–7), its belief that this was somehow an incomparable or exceptional act of violence (*DR!*, 49, 125–6, 137), the displacement of a proper political analysis and its effects on to a simplistic 'war against terrorism' (*DR!*, 107–8, 149–50).

In the present circumstances, as Žižek argues, we have no real choice: all alternatives are fundamentally the same. As he writes in *Welcome to the Desert of the Real!* of the supposed choice between 'terrorism' and the 'war against terrorism': 'Precisely in such moments of apparent clarity of choice, mystification is total. The choice proposed to us is not the true choice' (*DR!*, 54). And, indeed, what Žižek calls *terrorism* is just this rush towards the existing alternatives, in order not to face the true act that would break with the current symbolic order. That is, with regard to Kosovo, Žižek seeks to avoid the 'double blackmail' of the choice between the 'New World Order [of NATO intervention] and the neo-racist nationalists opposing it' ('DB', 82). With regard to 11 September, he rejects the choice between the simple 'condemnation [of the hijackers' motives] and the blatantly ideological assertion of American innocence' and the exculpatory analysis of the alleged 'deeper socio-political causes of Arab extremism [as though that excuses what happened] and the argument that America ultimately got what it deserved' (*DR!*, 50). But if we are only able to think the least 'bad' option here, the role of critical thinking is to open up another choice, to show that the existing alternatives are not exclusive, that there is another option that our current 'forced choice' stands in for and excludes. This is not merely to play the 'middle-man', who seeks to demonstrate that both alternatives are too extreme and aims to steer a more moderate course between them ('HR', 14). Rather, the task of a proper political analysis of a situation is to demonstrate that there *is* no neutral position, that we are always implicated in an ongoing struggle (*DR!*, 57), that we are always forced to take sides. And yet what we must also attempt to do *is* to speak for this universal, to think what in being excluded produces these choices, ensures that we are only able to take one of two sides ('HR', 23). That is, if we are only ever able to express this universality in terms of the currently existing symbolic horizon – as Žižek says that we can only speak of 'extending the war against terror' to America itself (*DR!*, 125–6) – it is also a matter of thinking what is left out from this, what other possibility allows this 'universality', why this 'universality' is not yet truly universal.

What are the consequences of all of this? As we say, it is not a matter of choosing between alternatives (or even, finally, of choosing an alternative that is not currently offered). This could only be a reflection of what is (Hegel's critique of Kant) or could only belong to the history of the victors (Benjamin's critique of historicism). But neither is it a matter of refusing to choose (in a way, we can only work within the existing choices; it is only by making a choice within the current system, by repeating the forced choice, that we are able to indicate what cannot be chosen). As we have tried to make clear, Žižek does not offer a coherent political and ethical programmme, able to be outlined in advance. He does not believe in a politics deriving from a 'universal' in this sense. On the contrary, his interventions are always specifically historical and contextually determined. Indeed, all that Žižek tells us is the *form* that such interventions must take. This, again, is the meaning of that 'form-alism' he speaks of (*L*, 189–90, 272, 312), which must be read in a 'Kan-tian' way: what Kant gives us in his ethics is not any particular content but only the *form* any particular political or ethical act must take. And for Žižek the form any proper political 'choice' must take is to 'maintain the fundamental choice' (*B*, 122). The act must point to, make visible, that antagonism which underlies all choices. And this 'formalism' can also be seen in those systems of thought so decisive to Žižek: Marxism and psychoanalysis. They offer no all-encompassing world-view; there is no identifiable programme or procedure they put forward in advance (despite some interpretations of them). And there is nothing outside of them, nothing they cannot speak of. Even their exception, resistance or contradiction is taken into account by them (*ME*, 181–3; *T?*, 228). In other words, it is because they offer not a specific content but only a certain 'form', speak not of something but only of that 'nothing' for which everything stands in, that they can only (and never properly) be followed. At once there is no exception to them and we can never exactly say what they are. They do not so much oppose anything to the world or propose some exception to it as introduce a certain 'split' into it.

To conclude here, does this not also apply to Žižek's whole system (and not just to his specific political determinations)? As his critics have pointed out, Žižek's entire project is nothing but a series of examples, is constantly directed by examples, seems almost to lose itself in its examples – examples which are understood philosophically as the very definition of what leads an argument astray (*TK*, 40–41). And yet at the same time, as has also been noted, we have the undoubted feeling that Žižek is always saying the 'same' thing; that no matter what he is actually talking about he always ends up making the 'identical' point. And, paradoxically – but this is the truth of all authentic philosophical systems – this endless 'saying', this absolute concern for specifics, is possible only because he *is* always saying the same thing. In that 'dialectic' of scientific method he speaks of (*K*, 25–7), Žižek precisely seeks to bring together the singular and the universal in his work. But, beyond this – and this is finally the most striking thing about reading him – this always saying the same thing is inseparable from the fact that Žižek is constantly contradicting himself, arguing against his own previous positions. As he admits, at least in this he is consistent. That is, in an exact replay of that ethical exercise of 'striking against oneself' (*L*, 226–7, 252–3), we have the absolutely uncanny sense that Žižek is saying the same thing not despite saying different things, or even despite the fact that he says contradictory things, but because he fundamentally *has nothing to say*.

What is this to suggest? How is all this like that 'act' we have been speaking of throughout? Alenka Zupančič in her *Ethics of the Real* theorizes the act as the attempt to bring together the example and the rule, description and prescription and enunciated and enunciation. And yet, as she says, it is this bringing together that exposes or produces the very *difference* between them. As she writes:

> It is possible to situate the act in another, inverse perspective [than the simple bringing together of statement and enunciation]: it is precisely the act, the ('successful') act, which fully discloses this splitting, makes it present. From this perspective, the definition of a successful act would be that it is structured exactly like the paradox of the liar: this structure is the same as the one evoked by the liar who says 'I am lying', who utters the impossible and thus fully displays the split between the level of the statement and the level of the enunciation, between the shifter 'I' and the signifier 'I am lying'.
> (*ER*, 103)

And when Žižek contradicts himself, admits he is wrong, he is effectively saying this 'I am lying.' That is, what Žižek is trying to bring about in his work – this is why Zupančič must be understood to be arguing not so much for the split between the enunciated and enunciation as for the final impossibility of bringing them together – is the equivalence of enunciated and enunciation: he is attempting to make its enunciation its enunciated. He is seeking to think that moment before the forced choice to enter the symbolic, before the 'fall of the binary signifier'. And yet it is always a question of a certain enunciation left out from *this*, like that shift from 'I' to 'I am lying.' At the same time as any equivalence is formed, another difference is brought about. We are always trying to think – this, again, is the subject as the continually upward journey to an 'ever higher Power' (*AF*, 85) – the (same) missing enunciation. The analyst – as opposed to the master – always endeavours to occupy this same (missing) position of enunciation (*B*, 109).

To put all this another way, with the 'collapse' of the distinction between enunciated and enunciation, the 'divine law and its sole support occupy the same level' (*ER*, 234). And *drive* is what emerges when the 'excluded object appears among other ("ordinary") objects' (*ER*, 244). And yet, in so far as the 'object on which [drive] leans' is always missing (*B*, 92), it is always a matter of what is excluded to allow this equivalence to be stated. It is just at this moment that we are forced to give up on our Cause, to say of any object: 'This is not it!' (*ER*, 244). And yet again – this is the 'splitting' that Cause induces – it is also at this point that we cannot but follow the Cause in its pure emptiness; the 'nothingness' of the Cause means that there is no exception to it. The Cause is always missing, but this *is* the Cause. It is at this point that the Cause becomes, as Zupančič says, 'oracular' (*ER*, 164), we might say, mathemic, Real. It is no longer a matter of anything enunciated but only of its enunciation – only an endless number of examples, 'more and more' – but all the more compelling for that. As opposed to desire, which is always characterized by a certain 'This is not that!', and which maintains the privilege therefore of always being proved by its own exception, drive is the impossible simultaneity of 'This is (not) that!', which is only the eternal antagonism of being the first exception to its own rule, the contradiction implied by the making equivalent of enunciated and enunciation. (This is also why it is not a matter of knowing in advance that we will fail to bring about this equivalence between enunciated and enunciation. It is not a matter of any fetishistic split, for this split is brought about only by this attempted equivalence.[8]) And this is the real way that the *Cause or drive of Theory* works. As Zupancic says, drive is what 'subtracts itself from the lack [of desire]' (*ER*, 242). That is to say, there is at once no lack in drive (versus desire) and drive is that lack for which the lack of desire only stands in (what makes the lack of desire possible). Drive is at once what is never missing, what cannot be avoided, and what is missing even when nothing is missing, what means that what is is already something else. Drive is not finally opposed to desire, but is that for which its 'other' or 'exception' stands in, what allows its 'inherent transgression'. In a sense, like this 'I am lying' or the dying woman's refusal of help, Žižek's whole aim is to pass beyond interpretation. With 'I am lying' there is no enunciation, no double meaning: its enunciation *is* its enunciated. And it is pure enunciation: there is always something left out of it. We might say that Žižek's theoretical Cause or drive – and here we refer not so much to Lacan as to Stephen King (*TK*, cvi–vii) – is that which 'does not stop (not) being written'.

Chapter 5

Žižek on others: others on Žižek

Thinking is never a matter of *criticism*, if we mean by that the objective statement of fact from a neutral, disengaged position. It does not argue with the other as though there is some verifiable 'reality' that exists outside of its symbolic construction. It does not dispute with them as though there is some 'Last Judgement' in which the truth of their respective claims would be decided. Rather, in an authentic act of criticism, we do not oppose the other, but bring out a certain 'internal' contradiction to them, repeat all that they are saying but for an entirely different reason. We do not pose an empirical objection to the other but propose the 'transcendental' conditions of their discourse: that which is in them 'more than themselves'. Now, this in the other 'more than themselves' can only return to them: our criticism can only seem to be what they are already saying; the other can already be seen to be responding to our criticism. But at the same time we might also try to think that what we are saying is *not* already in the other, that the other is *not* merely a reflection of our critical methods. And this is to suggest that there is something in the *relationship* of the critic to what they criticize that goes beyond both of them: that the critic is able to see something that is *not* already in the work; that the work is able to speak of something that is *not* already known to the critic. It is perhaps this relationship to the other that is the true creation of any significant theory, and that renders it permanently 'untimely', with any attempt to grasp it being either too soon or too late. To put this another way, as opposed to any timeless truth stated from an external perspective, the truth of any theory – as in 'Why is Every Act?' – exists only within its relationship to its interpreter and only during the very time of this relationship.

It is this that we see, for example, in the series of exchanges between Butler, Laclau and Žižek in the book *Contingency, Hegemony, Universality*. On the one hand, it is easy to dismiss each of the readings there as *misreadings*, as simply getting the facts wrong. (This is, in fact, what each of them accuses the others of doing.) On the other hand, we are only able to say this in the light of these readings, which if they seek to make their object over in their terms also allow us to see that it is *not* like this. But, beyond this, what is covered over by this series of mutual accusations, by this 'formal envelope' of errors, is that each is ultimately saying the 'same' thing. There is some issue in common to all of them that each at once is seen to embody and denies, accuses the others of and is accused of by others. But what could this be? On what basis could we bring together such apparent opposites as the deconstructionist feminist Butler, who argues for the parodic resignification of the Symbolic; the radical demo-crat Laclau, who argues for the progressive requilting of the social; and the Lacanian Marxist Žižek, who seemingly argues against both of these in favour of some unthinkable 'act' that would completely break with both the Symbolic and the social? What shared ground could there be between Butler, who accuses Žižek of a presumptive political logic that 'exceeds the instances of its exemplification' (*CHU*, 273); Laclau, who accuses Butler of a 'rigid opposition between structural determination and cultural specificity' (*CHU*, 189); and Žižek, who accuses Laclau of a Kantian 'resignation' in his theorization of a gap between the 'impos-sible Goal of a political engagement and its more modest realizable con-tent' (*CHU*, 316)?

There is thus a certain permanent 'antagonism' between the three participants in *Contingency, Hegemony, Universality*. It is more than a simple disagreement that would be external to the work, because it is an accusation that is made by each of them. And yet it is not simply inter-nal to the work, because it arises only in the relationship of each to the others. Rather, it is at once what each work needs to constitute itself, to allow it to speak to others, and what opens it up to the outside, allows others to speak of it. It is what we might call the relationship of the work to the other as *Real* (*CHU*, 213). That is, what we variously see in the dialogues of *Contingency, Hegemony, Universality* is the attempt of each interlocutor to constitute themselves by denying any relationship to the other (Imaginary), the attempt to take into account this relation-ship to the other (Symbolic) and the final impossibility of taking into account this relationship to the other (Real). What haunts each of them, what is that 'symptom' that each attempts to get rid of but cannot because it is what allows them, is their very relationship to the other, the fact that they are indistinguishable from the other. But, to consider this first of all from the point of view of Žižek, he in his dispute with Butler accuses her of a certain 'ahistoricism', in that, in her conception of a parodic re-enactment by the subject that would bring out the arbitrariness and constructedness of the Symbolic, there is nevertheless one thing that is not questioned – and that is the very relationship of this subject to the Symbolic. For all of her emphasis on performative self-transformation, she is ultimately proposing no more than an 'inherent transgression' within the Symbolic that would leave its essential terms unchanged. As Žižek writes:

> It is Butler who limits the subject's interventions to multiple resignifications/displacements of the basic 'passionate attachment', which therefore persists as the very limit/condition of subjectivity ... [For Butler,] it is possible to resignify/displace the 'symbolic substance' which predetermines my identity, but not totally to overhaul it, since a total exit would involve the psychotic loss of my symbolic identity. (*CHU*, 221–2)

Similarly, with regard to Laclau, Žižek argues that, although he is able to imagine the possibility of endless substitutions occurring within the current symbolic order, he is unable to think what makes this possible. That is, Žižek accuses Laclau of a certain 'formalism', in so far as there is a necessarily unquestioned background against which the struggle of competing master-signifiers proceeds. As he writes:

> [Butler and Laclau] both propose an abstract a priori formal model (of hegemony, of gender performativity ...) which allows, within its frame, for full contingency (no guarantee of what the outcome of the fight for hegemony will be, no last reference to the sexual constitution) ... Is not Laclau's theory of hegemony 'formalist' in the sense of proffering a certain a priori formal matrix of social space? There will always be some hegemonic empty signifier; it is only its content that shifts. (*CHU*, 111)

For their part, Butler and Laclau make almost identical criticisms of Žižek. Butler, echoing remarks she had previously made in her *Bodies that Matter*, accuses Žižek of 'ahistoricism', in so far as that 'Real' he argues she excludes is understood simply to lie outside of the Symbolic.[1] Typical of the 'essentialism' of psychoanalysis, with its fixed categories of the 'phallus' and 'fundamental lack', Žižek not only erects contingent historical conditions into timeless necessary ones but seeks to name what cannot properly be named. The two opposed sexes of classical psychoanalysis are not neutral or descriptive but implicitly normalize and canalize today's fluid, post-Oedipal sexual identities. As Butler writes:

If sexual difference enjoys this quasi-transcendental status, then all the concrete formulations of sexual difference (second-order forms of sexual difference) not only refer back to the more originary formulation but are, in their very expression, constrained by this non-thematizable normative condition. Thus, sexual difference operates as a radically incontestable principle or criterion that establishes intelligibility through foreclosure or, indeed, through pathologization or, indeed, through active political disenfranchisement. (*CHU*, 147)

Laclau too, in response to Žižek's criticisms of him not thinking what allows 'democratic' requilting to take place, in turn charges him with the very same 'formalism'. That is, when Žižek speaks of 'class' as what cannot be represented by the existing master-signifiers or as that prior exclusion against which contingent 'postmodern' subject-formation occurs, it is just this that should be open to hegemonic displacement. And, to the extent that Žižek is understood as not allowing this, he necessarily repeats either the 'transcendentalism' of Kant or the crudest oppositions of early Marxism. As Laclau writes:

Žižek moves within a new version of the base/superstructure model. There is a fundamental level on which capitalism proceeds according to its own logic, undisturbed by external influences, and a more superficial one where hegemonic articulations take place; the base operates as a framework, putting some sort of an a priori limit to what is historically achievable through mass action. (*CHU*, 292–3)

Žižek's reaction to these criticisms is that they radically misinterpret what he means by the 'Real'. First of all, in response to Butler's accusations concerning the 'ahistoricity' of the Real, he argues that not only is the Real not 'ahistorical' but it is the very thing that produces history. It is history itself that arises as the incessant attempt to come to terms with a certain traumatic Real. And, to avoid any further misunderstanding, he insists that the Real is not even to be seen as some unchanging substance that is left over after each attempted historicization. Rather, the Real just is that necessary point against which to mark this historicization, what makes what is this historicization, the repeated failure to come to terms with the Real. As Žižek writes against Butler:

Far from serving an implicit symbolic norm that reality can never reach, sexual difference as real/impossible means that *there is no such norm*: sexual difference is that 'rock of impossibility' on which every 'formalization' of sexual difference founders . . . If sexual difference may be said to be 'formal', it is certainly a strange form – a form whose main result is precisely that it undermines every universal form which attempts to capture it. (*CHU*, 309)

In the same way with Laclau, Žižek's point is that the 'class' he speaks of as underpinning the requilting of 'radical democracy' is not to be understood as some final hegemonization of the social field. In that case, either he would fall into the crudest forms of Marxism or this class would always be able to be requilted. Instead, Žižek's argument – as indicated by the very title of one of his responses, 'Class Struggle or Postmodernism? Yes, Please!' – is that it is ultimately not a matter of choosing between class and democracy. The contingent identities and 'floating signifiers' of postmodernism are the only way progressive politics can conduct itself today; but this is only possible because of class. And, again, this is not to be understood as saying that class is some unchanging element that comes before all of the others and that remains outside of them as their unspoken truth. In fact, class is no different from these others: it seeks to requilt other master-signifiers, as they seek to requilt it. But class is also what motivates this requilting, what necessitates that it will always be repeated (what can make us see what is as already repeated), in its perpetual failure to speak of class. As Žižek writes against Laclau:

> My point is *not* that the economy (the logic of capital) is a kind of 'essentialist anchor' that somehow 'limits' hegemonic struggle – on the contrary, it is its *positive condition*, the very background against which 'generalized hegemony' can thrive . . . This proliferation [of new political subjectivities], which seems to relegate 'class struggle' to a secondary role, is the result of 'class struggle'. (*CHU*, 319, 320)

We have here a series of mutually reflective arguments, with each party defending themselves against the same accusations they level at others. At first, Butler and Laclau condemn Žižek for a kind of 'ahistoricism' or 'formalism' (which can take the form either of an insufficiently interrogated transcendental category or an impossibly radical political project). In his defence, Žižek argues that this is not to understand that 'Real' he speaks of (which, far from being ahistorical and not subject to redefinition, precisely produces history and symbolic contingency). And, furthermore, he contends that it is in not adequately theorizing this Real that Butler and Laclau are themselves 'ahistorical' and 'formalist', in failing to think the very historicity of historicism or the conditionality of 'radical democracy'. But, in fact, the dispute is more complicated than this, which can still seem to be a question of individual error or inconsistency. For what is not yet seen – although it is occasionally hinted at by each of the participants – is that, in making these accusations of the others, each *necessarily* opens themselves up to the same accusation; that, in a manner familiar to us since the well-known debate around Edgar Allan Poe's 'The Purloined Letter', but at stake in philosophy since Hegel's critique of Kant, it is just in accusing the other of speaking of the transcendental that they *have* to do the same thing themselves.[2] This is the authentic 'Real' at stake in the debate in *Contingency, Hegemony, Universality*. It is not simply the psychoanalytic category of the 'Real' that Žižek mobilizes (and that the others in their way also lay claim to), but the very simultaneous necessity and impossibility of this gesture of naming the 'transcendental' conditions of the other: the fact that, in condemning the other for a certain 'ahistoricism' or 'formalism', each has to say what the true 'ahistorical' or 'formal' conditions of their naming are; that the reason the Real is not any transcendental outside of the Symbolic is because of a certain 'transcendental' outside of the Symbolic. This is the Real that is not merely the subject of each of the discourses but that is played out by each discourse, is that to which each discourse is subject.

It is with regard to *this* Real that we might properly assess each of the contributors to *Contingency, Hegemony, Universality*: to the extent to which they take this simultaneous necessity and impossibility into account. For example, we might consider here Žižek's insistence on a more profound 'exclusion' that precedes and makes possible those displacements and substitutions of Butler's historicism and Laclau's radical democracy. This raises the difficulty that in order to argue against their 'ahistoricism' or 'formalism' Žižek must himself name their 'ahistorical' or 'formal' conditions. As he writes, in a passage typical of several we have quoted:

> In order for this very struggle to take place, however, its *terrain* must constitute itself by means of a more fundamental exclusion ('primordial repression') that is not simply historical-contingent, a stake in the present constellation of the hegemonic struggle, since it *sustains the very terrain of historicity*. (*CHU*, 110)

And, as we say, this speaking of the transcendental conditions of the other is unavoidable; but the question here is, to what extent does Žižek go too far, forget that the 'Real' is also the *impossibility* of naming the transcendental conditions like this? That is, to what extent does Žižek forget that if we must distinguish between these two 'exclusions', the one empirical and the other transcendental, they also cannot be distinguished? To what extent does he think that this Real is only internal to the Symbolic, that this first exclusion is the only form this second can take (*CHU*, 120–21, 311)? And this is to say that any possible naming by Žižek of this second type of exclusion can only take the form of the first, can only be another resignification or requilting within the Symbolic. To give all this its final, paradoxical twist, Žižek at once accuses Butler and Laclau of failing to think a second, more profound, exclusion that cannot properly be thought, and in so doing repeats the same mistake of which he accuses them, of thinking an 'ahistoricist', 'formal' Real that is outside of the Symbolic.

However, as we say, if this problem arises in Žižek, it is only in so far as he is trying to avoid it. Indeed, as with all the other parties to the dialogue, we could ourselves no sooner accuse Žižek of making this mistake than he would already be seen to be responding to it. That is, on the one hand, Žižek criticizes Butler and Laclau for confusing two different levels of exclusion, for not seeking to imagine a 'completely different' (*CHU*, 223) political regime, for a Kantian refusal directly to embody their Ideas. And yet, on the other hand, it is Žižek who speaks of the way these two exclusions are unable to be distinguished (*CHU*, 215, 315), that we cannot think the outside of the Symbolic but only that empty signifier standing in for it (*CHU*, 112–14), that there is a 'dialectical tension' (*CHU*, 111) between the historical and the ahistorical. It is Žižek who speaks of the way it is a not a void that is subsequently filled in, but this void and its filling in are simultaneous (*CHU*, 109–10). It is Žižek who speaks of the way this 'primordially repressed' element 'gives body to [its own] loss' (*CHU*, 258). And this is why, finally, Žižek is able to say at the end of *Contingency, Hegemony, Universality* that it is not a question of thinking a 'completely different' order but of 'resignifying Terror' (*CHU*, 326), not a question of actually realizing this utopia but of this utopia making of everything a failure, the repetition of an always not taken choice (*CHU*, 324).

The simultaneity of the Real and the Symbolic

As we have tried to argue throughout, it is precisely Žižek's success in thinking this *simultaneity* of the empirical and the transcendental that is crucial to any evaluation of his work. It is the pressure of this simultaneity that we can see Žižek responding to in subtly shifting his position from book to book, and that makes of his entire oeuvre a forever unsuccessful act. It is this simultaneity that is the true Real at stake in it: at once the transcendental and the impossibility of the transcendental; that in response to which the Symbolic arises and only a deadlock within the Symbolic; a gap or void within the system and that which fills in this gap. And it is a Real that, as we have seen, makes of everything a 'not-all', suggesting a split not between things and that for which they 'stand in' (as in the Enlightenment and as Žižek's various interlocutors accuse him of in *Contingency, Hegemony, Universality*), but *between things and themselves*. In an extremely uncanny sense, things become their own failure, without our exactly being able to say what they fall short of. And this has the effect – again, the question of Žižek's exemplary method – both that everything is that exception for which everything stands in, that point around which the world turns, and nothing is, because we can never name this failure or exception to the Symbolic without it becoming merely another requilting or resignification within it (*L*, 267). However, at the same time – inseparable from the very attempt to think the Real – Žižek also *fails* to think this. He separates those two limits, those two exclusions, thus repeating the very split he seeks to overcome. He speaks of a void that exists before it is filled in, thus reverting to the masculine model of exception. He argues that we could actually manifest this 'completely different' political order, as though it would not always be seen as a failure, as a repetition of what has come before. (But, once more, the complexity of all of this – reminding us of that 'comedy' [*CHU*, 137] of mutual accusations we see in *Contingency, Hegemony, Universality* – is that, in accusing Žižek of this 'failure', it is not as though we could suggest ourselves how it should be done. Not only do we undoubtedly commit the same errors here in ways we cannot see, but the point we are trying to make is that no one could ever properly think this simultaneity in so far as it is Real. Indeed, in another sense – and, again, as opposed to Žižek's criticism of Butler and Laclau for failing to think it, as though it is simply some idea or essence that can simply be grasped – this very failure to think it *is* it, can only be explained *because of* it. That Real we are trying to describe is nothing *but* this failure, is what allows us to think that it *is* a failure. This Real exists nowhere else but in our very saying of it, nowhere else but in the very text and texture of Žižek's work.)

We have already spoken of this ambivalence or undecidability that runs throughout Žižek's work. We have noted such examples as Žižek's description of psychoanalysis as rendering visible the place 'in its original emptiness, i.e., as preceding the element which fills it out', in 'Why Is Every Act?'; his insistence on the possibility of images of trauma somehow 'gentrifying' the Real, as though we could ever say what it is outside of these, in *Fragile Absolute*; his opposition between idealism and materialism, in terms of whether it is a linguistic excess that arises as a deadlock within an already existing linguistic system or the linguistic system itself that arises in response to this excess, in *Indivisible Remainder*. And we can think of many other examples of this 'separation' throughout Žižek's work: his argument that the place logically 'precedes' the object that fills it (*SO*, 194); his distinction between the empty space in the Symbolic and the leftover object that occupies it (*ME*, 131; *FA*, 30); his assertion that the locus of power must be kept 'empty' in democracy (*SO*, 147; *TN*, 221); his understanding of the subject as a void 'before' or 'outside' of ideological interpellation (*TN*, 40; *TS*, 265); his split between a letter arriving and not arriving (*E!*, 9); the question of the status of that 'minimal difference' between an event and its historicization and the death-drive and its sublimation (*AF*, 38; *TS*, 160); the relationship, as in *Contingency, Hegemony, Universality*, between two 'negations', one occurring within the symbolic order and the other outside (*TS*, 158).

But at the same time there is also in Žižek the thinking of the simultaneity or inseparability of the empirical and the transcendental. (And, again, the fact that this is not a simple 'error' that is progressively eliminated, but that we can find instances of both this separation and putting together throughout his work, indicates the status of this problematic as a kind of 'Real' within it.) For example, as early as *Sublime Object*, we have Žižek thinking the Real as both what precedes the Symbolic and what arises only within it (*SO*, 169–70). In *For They Know Not*, we have Žižek speaking of the way that with regard to the Symbolic re-mark, the 'place' of the inscription of the marks is 'nothing but the void opened up by the failure of the re-mark' (*TK*, 86). In *Ticklish Subject*, we have Žižek saying that that 'universal' empty space is always 'coloured' by a particular pathological content (*TS*, 277). In *Fragile Absolute*, we have Žižek admitting that this empty place never 'takes place' as such, but only as a retrospective effect of it being filled in (*FA*, 31). In *Totalitarianism?*, we have Žižek's critique of deconstructionist messianism which wants to have the matrix of the religious without the God that sustains it (*T?*, 153). In *Revolution at the Gates*, we have Žižek insisting against Dominick La Capra that we cannot make a distinction between a contingent, historical trauma and that deeper, ontological one for which it might be understood to stand in (*L*, 314). And, finally, there is the whole series of 'infinite judgements' that runs throughout Žižek's work, which are also an attempt to capture that 'Real' of the simultaneity of the empirical and the transcendental, the world and what it 'stands in' for: appearance *is* the supersensible (*SO*, 193; *TN*, 196); essence *is* non-essentialist (*ME*, 159); the master-signifier *is* a supplement (*ME*, 196); the phallus *is* its own absence (ME, 202); immanence *is* transcendence (*IR*, 171); conformity *is* subversive (*L*, 262); resemblance *is* non-identity (*FA*, 50); man *is* God (*TS*, 231; *B*, 97); the current positive order *is* its own negation (*TS*, 234); and the possible *is* impossible (*TS*, 98–9; *L*, 274–5).

However, as we have said, each of our examples is ambiguous here. It is arguable that even in these negative cases Žižek is attempting to think this simultaneity, is posing the separation of the empirical and the transcendental only to overcome it. It can be seen that, in speaking against the transcendentality of others, he necessarily has to say what the transcendental is *not*. Finally, it is not a mistake because this 'gap' (not equivalence) implied by the simultaneity of the empirical and the transcendental is itself a form of transcendentality. *This simultaneity of the empirical and the transcendental is itself the transcendental.*[3] And, again, we would insist that it is not just we who see this complex logic as central to Žižek's project, but Žižek himself. It is this simultaneity, as the simultaneity of the empirical and the transcendental, the enunciated and its enunciation, the exception and what it stands in for, that we understand as the fundamental topic throughout Žižek's work. But – and this is to connect 'Why is Every Act?' to the debates of *Contingency, Hegemony, Universality* – we could no sooner speak of this than lose it, allow another to pose the question of that transcendentality or enunciation that makes *this* simultaneity possible. However, following Zupancic's remarks in our previous chapter, it is not simply a matter of thinking this transcendentality as impossible, as failed in advance, for *it comes about only as the retrospective effect of the attempt to think it.* This is the meaning of Žižek's exhortation to 'Demand the impossible!' (*CHU*, 321), to imagine a 'completely different' political reality, even though he 'knows' this is impossible. But, more profoundly, it is the very strength and unity of his work that there *is* this 'contradiction' or 'impossibility' played out in it, as opposed to the 'deconstructive' attempt to avoid this by way of an incessant reflection on this impossibility. It is precisely what Žižek advocates as the 'metalanguage' of all authentic philosophy: this attempt to make the empirical and the transcendental, the enunciated and its enunciation, the same; and, in the failure to do so, opening up that transcendental or enunciation that would allow this to be noted (a transcendental or enunciation that would be itself unthinkable outside of some empirical or enunciated). As Žižek writes, using the very same example of 'I am lying' as Zupančič: 'From the Lacanian perspective, it is, on the contrary, precisely such impossible utterances — utterances following the logic of the paradox "I am lying" — which keep the fundamental gap of the signifying process open and in this way prevent us from assuming a metalanguage position' (*SO*, 156). And this is the truly compelling thing about Žižek's work, its ethical, 'self-beating' aspect. It is the way its metastatement 'I am lying' ultimately becomes 'I am telling the truth' (*E*, 121).

It is in this sense — not so much in what it says as in its saying, not so much in its content as in its form — that Žižek's work is *critical*. As we saw in the previous chapter, it is not critical in the sense of laying out a coherent political and economic analysis. It is not critical in the sense that it does away with the symbolic order or thinks identity outside of the Other. (This is the objection of someone like the Frankfurt School philosopher Peter Dews, who argues that, despite his professed left-wing stance, Žižek is in fact conservative in giving us 'no philosophical reason to assume that the dismal cycle of abstract, universalist expansion and particularist contraction should ever be progressively attenuated or overcome'.)[4] And it is true: Žižek *does* only repeat the problems he analyses. There is an absolute identification of his work with the world, so that it can sometimes be mistaken for it (the risk of all post-Enlightenment philosophy). But — this could seem only a paltry compensation for someone like Dews, who wants concrete 'solutions' — we would say that not only does Žižek repeat those problems he analyses, but that these are not even problems until he repeats them. And it is this logic of the 'forced choice' that is played out in Žižek's work. As opposed to the false distance of the 'inherent transgression' of criticism, which operates as though there is some Big Other to accuse, or as though there is some external standard of truth to appeal to, it is only through an absolute identification with the system that we realize that it does not exist until us. At once there is no outside to the system and the system becomes its own outside, forever driven to expand to catch up with that act that originally made it possible (*TN*, 209–10). 'Criticism' therefore is no longer to be thought of in terms of contradiction or exception, but as what renders what is 'not-all'. This is the true 'infinite judgement' in Žižek, along the lines of 'The state is the King' or 'The Spirit is a Bone': capitalism *is* its criticism by Žižek or the problem *is* its solution (*TN*, 93–4). And this is to suggest again that the 'meaning' of Žižek's work lies not in anything he actually says but in that very 'positing', enunciation, by which he 'contracts' with what is. This is the real critical 'act' of the work – this act of repeating what is.

It is for *this* reason, finally, that Žižek can hold up the possibility of a 'completely different' social organization, can argue that only a utopian would not think that there will be a total revolution. It is not that these things will actually come to pass or that we can somehow bring them about. In fact, they will never come to pass, we cannot bring them about – and even if we could, either we would not be ready for them or they could only be seen as a repetition of what came before. But Žižek is right because the current order as it is can only be explained because of them. To return to the issues of *Contingency, Hegemony, Universality*, we might say that they are that 'Real' to which what is responds. And, crucially – this is the other objection that might be made of Žižek here – this is not at all to rule out concrete social and political action, which would be seen as futile, merely the substitute for the 'real' thing. Rather, the very actuality of what is, the fact that there is no alternative to what takes place in the present, is only possible because of the 'Real' of this 'completely different' order, this 'utopia' that marks the failure of every 'universal' project, ensures that there is only ever the 'particular'. [5] To put this another way, in any making equivalent of the empirical and the transcendental, there is always something left out: that 'transcendental' point, that place of enunciation, from which this is re-marked. The world as it is – this, again, is Žižek's essential conception of philosophy as 'transcendental' (*TN*, 2–5) – is only possible because of something else. And philosophy as transcendental' philosophy, as the thinking of the 'discourse's frame', is the story of this always repeated attempt to take this enunciation into account. The history of philosophy progresses as the always more and more refined taking into account of what is missing from what comes before to allow it to be 'all'; the essential subject of philosophy (as both its subject matter and the great names that make it up) is the 'predicate of an ever higher power' (*AF*, 85). And yet at the same time it is the 'same' world we begin with; it is always the 'same' problem, the 'same' impossible simultaneity of the empirical and the transcendental, the enunciated and its enunciation.

Indeed, in perhaps the most polemical gesture of all here, we would precisely *not* make a distinction – despite his repeated assertions – between Žižek and his post-structuralist contemporaries in this regard. Rather, all philosophers of 'system' – this is what is brought out in the debates of *Contingency, Hegemony, Universality* – are involved in the same problem of thinking the simultaneous necessity and impossibility of the transcendental. They are all engaged in the same post-Enlightenment problem of showing how the world as it is is possible only because of an always excluded enunciation or re-mark. It is not an alternative to the world that they offer, but a re-marking of that place from where there is no alternative. All significant thinking is thus engaged with the problem of the 'forced choice': it is only in thinking that there is no alternative to what is that some alternative is opened up. Any actual alternative could only stand in for this transcendental one, and this is what ensures that there is no transcendental alternative but only the actual. And all significant philosophy is this *drive*: at once the thinking that there is nothing missing from what is and in the very thinking of this the production of a certain 'excess' or 'gap' (*B*, 92–5). This is philosophy again as the 'subjectivizing' of substance and as a history of 'subjects', re-marked repetitions of the 'same' enunciated. As Nietzsche – undoubtedly one of the first philosophers in his notion of the Eternal Return to conceive of philosophy as this 'forced choice' – once said: 'All the names of history are me.' That is, if Žižek is to be a true philosopher, if he is to join in its 'dialogue', then he must repeat everything that comes before him unchanged and everything must become 'Žižekian'.

Chapter 6

Žižek live

Slavoj Žižek, could you say something about Judaism and Christianity and how guilt and the superego are understood in each?

Let us begin by considering the Jewish prohibition of images. The Jewish commandment that prohibits images of God is the obverse of the statement that relating to one's neighbour is the *only* terrain of religious practice, where the divine dimension is present in our lives – 'No images of God' does not point towards a gnostic experience of the divine beyond our reality, a divine that is beyond any image; on the contrary, it designates a kind of ethical *hic Rhodus, hic salta*: you want to be religious? OK, prove it *here*, in the 'works of love', in the way you relate to your neighbours . . . We have here a nice case of the Hegelian reversal of reflexive determination into determinate reflection: instead of saying 'God is love', we should say 'love is divine' (and, of course, the point is not to conceive of this reversal as the standard humanist platitude). It is for this precise reason that Christianity, far from standing for a regression towards an image of God, only draws the consequence of the Jewish iconoclasm through asserting the identity of God and man. And it is this very identity that compels us to render problematic the notion of grace. In Mozart's *La Clemenza di Tito*, just before the final pardon, Tito himself exasperates at the proliferation of treasons which oblige him to proliferate acts of clemency:

> The very moment that I absolve one criminal, I discover another . . .
> I believe the stars conspire to oblige me, in spite of myself, to become
> cruel. No: they shall not have this satisfaction. My virtue has
> already pledged itself to continue the contest. Let us see which is
> more constant, the treachery of others or my mercy . . . Let it be
> known to Rome that I am the same and that I know all, absolve
> everyone, and forget everything.

One can almost hear Tito complaining: *Uno per volta, per carita!* ('Please, not so fast, one after the other, in the line for mercy!') Living up to his task, Tito forgets everyone, but those whom he pardons are condemned to remember it forever:

SEXTUS: It is true, you pardon me, Emperor; but my heart will not absolve me; it will lament the error until it no longer has memory.
TITUS: The true repentance of which you are capable, is worth more than constant fidelity.

This couplet from the finale blurts out the obscene secret of *clemenza*: the pardon does not really abolish the debt, it rather makes it infinite – we are *forever* indebted to the person who pardoned us. No wonder Tito prefers repentance to fidelity: in fidelity to the Master, I follow him out of respect, while in repentance, what attached me to the Master is the infinite indelible guilt. In this, Tito is a thoroughly Christian master.

Usually, it is Judaism which is conceived as the religion of the superego (of man's subordination to the jealous, mighty and severe God), in contrast to the Christian God of Mercy and Love – one opposes the Jewish rigorous Justice and the Christian Mercy, the inexplicable gesture of undeserved pardon: we, humans, were born in sin, we cannot ever repay our debts and redeem ourselves through our own acts – our only salvation lies in God's Mercy, in His supreme sacrifice. However, in this very gesture of breaking the chain of Justice through the inexplicable act of Mercy, of paying our debt, Christianity imposes on us an even stronger debt: we are forever indebted to Christ, we cannot ever repay him for what he did for us. The Freudian name for such an excessive pressure that we cannot ever remunerate is, of course, superego. It is precisely through *not* demanding from us the price of our sins, through paying this price for us Himself, that the Christian God of Mercy establishes Himself as the supreme superego agency: 'I paid the highest price for your sins, and you are thus indebted to me *forever* ...' Is this God as the superego agency, Whose very Mercy generates the indelible guilt of believers, the ultimate horizon of Christianity? One should effectively correlate the superego unconditional guilt and the mercy of love – two figures of the excess, the excess of guilt without proportion to what I effectively did and the excess of mercy without proportion to what I deserve on account of my acts.

As such, the dispensation of mercy is the most efficient constituent of the exercise of power. That is to say, is the relationship between law (legal justice) and mercy really the one between necessity and choice?

Is it really that one *has* to obey the law, while mercy is by definition dispensed as a free and excessive act, as something that the agent of mercy is free to do or not to do – mercy under compulsion is no mercy but, at its best, a travesty of mercy? What if, at a deeper level, the relationship is the opposite one? What if, with regard to law, we have the freedom to choose (to obey or violate it), while mercy is obligatory, we *have* to display it – mercy is an unnecessary excess which, as such, *has* to occur. (And does the law not always take into account this freedom of ours, not only by punishing us for its transgression but by providing escapes to being punished by its ambiguity and inconsistency?) Is it not that showing mercy is the *only* way for a Master to demonstrate his supralegal authority? If a Master were merely to guarantee the full application of the law, of legal regulations, he would be deprived of his authority and turn into a mere figure of knowledge, the agent of the discourse of the university.

OK, could you tell us a little about this discourse of the university and its relationship to that of the Master? Isn't your point that it needs it?

Lacan provides the answer to this in his *L'Envers de la psychanalyse*, his seventeenth Seminar (1969–70) on the four discourses, his response to the events of 1968 – its premise is best captured as his reversal of the well-known anti-structuralist graffito from the Paris walls of 1968, 'Structures do not walk on the streets!': if anything, this Seminar endeavours to demonstrate how structures *do* walk on the streets, i.e., how structural shifts *can* account for social outbursts like that of 1968. Instead of the one symbolic order with its set of a priori rules which guarantee social cohesion, we get the matrix of the passages from one to another discourse: Lacan's interest is focused on the passage from the discourse of the Master to the discourse of university as the hegemonic discourse in contemporary society. No wonder that the revolt was located at the universities: as such, it merely signalled the shift to the new forms of domination in which the scientific discourse serves to legitimize the relations of domination. Lacan's underlying premise is sceptical-conservative – his diagnosis is best captured by his famous retort to the student revolutionaries: 'As hysterics, you demand a new master. You will get one!' This passage can also be conceived in more general terms, as the passage from the pre-revolutionary *ancien régime* to the post-revolutionary new Master who does not want to admit that he is one, but proposes himself as a mere 'servant' of the People. In Nietzsche's terms, it is simply the passage from a Master's ethics to slave morality; and this fact, perhaps, enables us [to adopt] a new approach to Nietzsche: when Nietzsche scornfully dismisses 'slave morality', he is not attacking the lower classes as such, but rather the new masters who are no longer ready to assume the title of the Master – 'slave' is Nietzsche's term for a fake master. How, then, more closely, are we to read the university discourse? To represent it diagrammatically:

$$\frac{S2}{S1} \frac{a}{\$}$$

The university discourse is enunciated from the position of 'neutral' Knowledge; it addresses the remainder of the real (say, in the case of pedagogical knowledge, the 'raw, uncultivated child'), turning it into the subject ($\$$). The 'truth' of the university discourse, hidden beneath the bar, of course, is power, i.e., the master-signifier: the constitutive lie of the university discourse is that it disavows its performative dimension, presenting what effectively amounts to a political decision based on power as a simple insight into the factual state of things. What one should avoid here is the Foucauldian misreading: the produced subject is not simply the subjectivity that arises as a result of the disciplinary application of knowledge-power, but its remainder, that which eludes the grasp of knowledge-power. 'Production' (the fourth term in the matrix of discourses) does not stand simply for the result of the discursive operation, but rather for its 'indivisible remainder', for the excess that resists being included in the discursive network, i.e., for what the discourse itself produces as the foreign body in its very heart. And, yes, perhaps the exemplary case of the Master's position which underlies the university discourse is the way in which medical discourse functions in our everyday lives: at the surface-level, we are dealing with pure objective knowledge which desubjectivizes the subject-patient, reducing him to an object of research, of diagnosis and treatment; however, beneath it, one can easily discern a worried hystericized subject, obsessed with anxiety, addressing the doctor as his Master and asking for reassurance from him. At a more common level, suffice it to recall the market expert who advocates strong budgetary measures (cutting welfare expenses, etc.) as a necessity imposed by his neutral expertise devoid of any ideological biases: what he conceals is the series of power-relations (from the active role of state apparatuses to ideological beliefs) which sustain the 'neutral' functioning of the market mechanism.

In the university discourse, is not the upper level (S2 → a) that of biopolitics (in the sense deployed from Foucault to Agamben)? Of the expert knowledge dealing with its object, which is *a* – not subjects, but individuals reduced to bare life? And does the lower level not designate what Eric Santner called the 'crisis of investiture', i.e., the impossibility of the subject to relate to S1, to identify with a master-signifier, to assume the imposed symbolic mandate?[1] The key point is here that the expert rule of 'biopolitics' is grounded in and conditioned by the crisis of investiture; this crisis generated the 'post-metaphysical' survivalist stance of the Last Men, which ends up in the anaemic spectacle of life dragging on as its own shadow. It is within this horizon that one should appreciate today's growing rejection of death-penalty: what one should be able to discern is the hidden 'biopolitics' that sustains this rejection. Those who assert the 'sacredness of life', defending it against the threat of transcendent powers which parasitize on it, end up in a world in which, on behalf of its very official goal – long pleasurable life – all effective pleasures are prohibited or strictly controlled (smoking, drugs, food ...). Spielberg's *Saving Private Ryan* is the latest example of this survivalist attitude towards dying, with its 'demystifying' presentation of war as a meaningless slaughter that nothing can really justify – as such, it provides the best possible justification for the Colin Powell 'no-casualties-on-our-side' military doctrine.

In today's market, we find a whole series of products deprived of their malignant property: coffee without caffeine, cream without fat, beer without alcohol ... And the list goes on: what about virtual sex as sex without sex, the Colin Powell doctrine of warfare with no casualties (on our side, of course) as warfare without warfare, the contemporary redefinition of politics as the art of expert administration as politics without politics, up to today's tolerant liberal multiculturalism as an experience of the Other deprived of its Otherness (the idealized Other who dances fascinating dances and has an ecologically sound holistic approach to reality, while features like wife-beating remain out of sight ...)? Virtual Reality simply generalizes this procedure of offering a product deprived of its substance: it provides reality itself deprived of its substance, of the resisting hard kernel of the Real – in the same way decaffeinated coffee smells and tastes like the real coffee without being the real one, Virtual Reality is experienced as reality without being one.

Do we not have here yet another example of this 'coincidence of opposites'? And what is the possibility of an authentic 'act' in these circumstances?

Yes, today's hedonism combines pleasure with constraint – it is no longer the old notion of the 'right measure' between pleasure and constraint, but a kind of pseudo-Hegelian immediate coincidence of opposites:

action and reaction should coincide, the very thing which causes damage should already be the medicine. The ultimate example of this is arguably a *chocolate laxative*, available in the USA, with the paradoxical injunction 'Do you have constipation? Eat more of this chocolate!', i.e., of the very thing that causes constipation. Do we not find here a weird version of Wagner's famous 'Only the spear which caused the wound can heal it' from *Parsifal*? And is not a negative proof of the hegemony of this stance the fact that true unconstrained consumption (in all its main forms: drugs, free sex, smoking ...) is emerging as the main danger? The fight against these dangers is one of the main investments of today's 'biopolitics'. Solutions are here desperately sought which would reproduce the paradox of the chocolate laxative. The chief contender is 'safe sex' − a term which makes one appreciate the truth of the old saying 'Is having sex with a condom not like taking a shower with a raincoat on?' The ultimate goal would be here, along the lines of decaf coffee, to invent 'opium without opium': no wonder marijuana is so popular among liberals who want to legalize it − it already *is* a kind of 'opium without opium'.

Superego in all these cases is thus not directly S1; it is rather the S1 of the S2 itself, the dimension of an unconditional injunction that is inherent to knowledge itself. Recall the warnings about health we are bombarded with all the time: 'Smoking is dangerous! Too much fat may cause a heart attack! Regular exercise leads to a longer life!' etc., etc. − it is impossible not to hear beneath all this the unconditional injunction 'You should enjoy a long and healthy life!' What this means is that the discourse of the university is thoroughly mystifying, concealing its true foundation, obfuscating the unfreedom on which it relies.

Within this horizon, the concept of radical, 'unrepresentable' Evil, be it the Holocaust or gulag, plays the central role, that of the constitutive limit and point of reference of today's predominant notion of democracy: 'democracy' means avoiding the 'totalitarian' extreme, it is defined as a permanent struggle against the 'totalitarian' temptation to close the gap, to (pretend to) act on behalf of the Thing itself. Ironically, it is thus as if one should turn around the well-known Augustinian notion of Evil as having no positive substance or force of its own, but being just the absence of Good: Good itself is the absence of Evil, the distance towards the Evil Thing.

It is this liberal blackmail of dismissing every radical political act as evil that one should thoroughly reject − even when it is coated in Lacanian colours, as is the case in Yannis Stavrakakis's recent critical reply to my reading of *Antigone*, which focuses on the danger of what he calls the 'absolutization' of the event, which then leads to a totalitarian *désastre*. When Stavrakakis writes that 'fidelity to an event can flourish and avoid absolutization only as an infidel fidelity, only within the framework of another fidelity, fidelity to the openness of the political space and to the awareness of the constitutive impossibility of a final suture of the social', he thereby surreptitiously introduces a difference, which can be given different names, between the unconditional-ethical and the pragmatico-political: the original fact is the lack, opening, which pertains to human finitude, and all positive acts always fall short of this primordial lack; we have thus what Derrida calls the unconditional ethical injunction, impossible to fulfil, and positive acts, interventions, which remain strategic interventions ... One should evoke two arguments against this position:

(1) 'Acts' in Lacan's sense precisely suspend this gap – they are 'impossible' not in the sense of 'impossible *to* happen', but in the sense of 'impossible *that* happened'. *This* is why Antigone was of interest to me: her act is not a strategic intervention that maintains the gap towards the impossible Void – it rather tends to 'absolutely' enact the Impossible. I am well aware of the 'lure' of such an act – but I claim that, in Lacan's later versions of the act, this moment of 'madness' beyond strategic intervention remains. In this precise sense, the notion of act not only does not contradict the 'lack in the Other' which, according to Stavrakakis, I neglect – it directly presupposes it: it is only through an act that I effectively assume the big Other's inexistence, i.e., I enact the impossible, namely what appears as impossible within the coordinates of the existing sociosymbolic order.

(2) There *are* (also) political acts, i.e., politics cannot be reduced to the level of strategic-pragmatic interventions. In a radical political act, the opposition between a 'crazy' destructive gesture and a strategic political decision momentarily breaks down – which is why it is theoretically and politically wrong to oppose strategic political acts, as risky as they can be, to radical 'suicidal' gestures *à la* Antigone, gestures of pure self-destructive ethical insistence with, apparently, no political goal. The point is not simply that once we are thoroughly engaged in a political project we are ready to put at stake everything for it, inclusive of our lives, but, more precisely, that *only such an 'impossible' gesture of pure expenditure can change the very coordinates of what is strategically possible within a historical constellation.* This is the key point: an act is neither a strategic intervention *into* the existing order, nor its 'crazy' destructive *negation*; an act is an 'excessive', trans-strategic, intervention which redefines the rules and contours of the existing order.

So what about the reproach that Antigone does not only risk death or suspend the symbolic order – my determination of a political act – but that she actively strives for death, for symbolic and real death, thereby displaying a purity of desire beyond any sociopolitical transformative action? First, is Antigone's act really outside politics, 'apolitical'? Is not her defiance to the order of the supreme power (Creon, who acts on behalf of the common good) political, albeit in a negative way? Is not, in certain extreme circumstances, such 'apolitical' defiance on behalf of 'decency' or 'old customs' even the very model of heroic political resistance? Second, her gesture is not simply pure desire for death – to do that, she could have directly killed herself and spared the people around her all the fuss ... hers was not a pure symbolic striving for death but an unconditional insistence on a particular symbolic ritual.

And this brings us to the key dilemma: what the reference to democracy involves is the rejection of the radical attempts to 'step outside', to risk a radical break, to pursue the trend of self-organized collectives in areas outside the law. Arguably the greatest literary monument to such a utopia comes from an unexpected source – Mario Vargas Llosa's *The War of the End of the World* (1981), the novel about Canudos, an outlaw community deep in the Brazilian backlands which was a home to prostitutes, freaks, beggars, bandits and the most wretched of the poor. Canudos, led by an apocalyptic prophet, was a utopian space without money, property, taxes and marriage. In 1897 it was destroyed by the military forces of the Brazilian government. The echoes of Canudos are clearly discernible in today's *favelas* in Latin American megalopolises: are they, in some sense, not the first 'liberated territories', the cells of future self-organized societies? Are institutions like community kitchens not a model of 'socialized' communal local life? The Canudos liberated territory in Bahia will remain forever the model of a liberated space, of an alternative community that thoroughly negates the existing state space. Everything is to be endorsed here, up to the religious 'fanaticism'. It is as if, in such communities, *the Benjaminian other side of the historical Progress, the defeated ones, acquire a space of their own*. Utopia *existed* here for a brief period of time – this is the only way to account for the 'irrational', excessive, violence of the destruction of these communities. (In Brazil in 1897, *all* the inhabitants of Canudos, children and women included, were slaughtered, as if the very memory of the possibility of freedom had to be erased – and this by a government which presented itself as 'progressive' liberal-democratic-republican ...) Till now, such communities exploded from time to time as passing phenomena, as sites of eternity that interrupted the flow of temporal progress – one should have the courage to recognize them in the wide span from the Jesuit *reducciones* in eighteenth-century Paraguay (brutally destroyed by the joint action of Spanish and Portuguese armies) up to the settlements controlled by Sendero Luminoso (Shining Path guerrillas) in Peru of the 1990s. There is a will to accomplish the 'leap of faith' and *step out* of the global circuit that is at work here, the will whose extreme and terrifying expression is the well-known incident from the Vietnam War: after the US Army occupied a local village, their doctors vaccinated the children on their left arm in order to demonstrate their humanitarian care; when, the day later, the village was retaken by Vietcong, they cut off the left arm of all the vaccinated children ... although difficult to sustain as a literal model to follow, this thorough rejection of the Enemy precisely in its helping 'humanitarian' aspect, no matter what the costs, has to be endorsed in its basic intention. In a similar way, when Sendero Luminoso took over a village, they did not focus on killing the soldiers or policemen stationed there, but more on the UN or US agricultural consultants or health-workers trying to help the local peasants – after lecturing them for hours and then forcing them to confess publicly their complicity with imperialism, they shot them. Brutal as this procedure was, it was sustained by the correct insight: they, not the police or the army, were the true danger, the enemy at its most perfidious, since they were 'lying in the guise of truth' – the more they were 'innocent' (they 'really' tried to help the peasants), the more they served as a tool of the USA. It is only such a strike against the enemy at his best, at the point where the enemy 'indeed helps us', that displays a true revolutionary autonomy and 'sovereignty' (to use this term in its Bataillean meaning). If one adopts the attitude of 'let us take from the enemy what is good and reject or even fight against what is bad', one is already caught in the liberal trap of 'humanitarian help'.

In other words, one targets the Master precisely at that moment of mercy by which he empowers himself?

Yes, but to go back to what we were saying, since, today, capitalism defines and structures the totality of the human civilization, every 'communist' territory was and is – again, in spite of its horrors and failures – a kind of 'liberated territory', as Fred Jameson put it apropos of Cuba. What we are dealing with here is the old structural notion of the gap between the Space and the positive content that fills it in: although, as to their positive content, the communist regimes were mostly a dismal failure, generating terror and misery, they at the same time opened up a certain space, the space of utopian expectations which, among other things, enabled us to measure the failure of really existing socialism itself. (What the anti-communist dissidents as a rule tend to overlook is that the very space from which they themselves criticized and denounced the everyday terror and misery was opened and sustained by the communist breakthrough, by its attempt to escape the logic of Capital.) This is how one should understand Alain Badiou's *mieux vaut un désastre qu'un désêtre*, so shocking for the liberal sensitivity: better the worst Stalinist terror than the most liberal capitalist democracy. Of course, the moment one compares the positive content of the two, welfare-state capitalist democracy is incomparably better – what re-deems Stalinist 'totalitarianism' is the formal aspect, the *space* it opens up. Can one imagine a utopian point at which this subterranean level of the utopian Other Space would unite with the positive space of 'normal' social life? The key political question is here: is there in our 'postmodern' time still a space for such communities? Are they limited to the undeveloped outskirts (*favelas*, ghettos), or is a space for them emerging in the very heart of the 'postindustrial' landscape? Can one make a wild wager that the dynamics of 'postmodern' capitalism with its rise of new eccentric geek communities provides a new chance here? That, perhaps for the first time in history, the logic of alternative com-munities can be grafted onto the latest state of technology?

And how would we begin to answer such a question?

First of all, things are not so straightforward. On the one hand, direct democracy is not only still alive in many places like *favelas*, it is even being 'reinvented' and given a new boost by the rise of the 'postindus-trial' digital culture (do the descriptions of the new 'tribal' communities of computer-hackers not often evoke the logic of councils-democracy?). On the other hand, the awareness that politics is a complex game in which a certain level of institutional alienation is irreducible should not lead us to ignore the fact that there is still a line of separation which divides those who are 'in' from those who are 'out', excluded from the space of the *polis* – there are citizens, and there is the spectre of *homo sacer* haunting them all. In other words, even 'complex' contemporary societies still rely on the basic divide between included and excluded. The fashionable notion of 'multitude' is insufficient precisely in so far as it cuts across this divide: there is a multitude *within* the system and the multitude of those *excluded*, and simply to encompass them within the scope of the same notion amounts to the same obscenity as equating starvation with dieting to lose weight. And those excluded do not simply dwell in a psychotic non-structured Outside – they have (and are forced into) their own self-organization, one of the names (and practices) of which was precisely the 'council-democracy'.

But should we still call it 'democracy'? At this point, it is crucial to avoid what one cannot but call the 'democratic trap'. Many 'radical' Leftists accept the legalistic logic of the 'transcendental guarantee': they refer to 'democracy' as the ultimate guarantee of those who are aware that there is no guarantee. That is to say, since no political act can claim a direct foundation in some transcendent figure of the big Other (of the 'we are just instruments of a higher Necessity or Will' type), since every such act involves the risk of a contingent decision, nobody has the right to impose his choice on others – which means that every collective choice has to be democratically legitimized. From this perspective, democracy is not so much the guarantee of the right choice as a kind of opportunistic insurance against possible failure: if things turn out wrong, I can always say we are all responsible … Consequently, this last refuge must be dropped; one should fully assume the risk. The only adequate position is the one advocated already by Lukács in his *History and Class Consciousness*: democratic struggle should not be fetishized; it is one of the forms of struggle, and its choice should be determined by a global strategic assessment of circumstances, not by its ostensibly superior intrinsic value. Like the Lacanian analyst, a political agent has to commit acts which can only be authorized by themselves, for which there is no external guarantee.

An authentic political act can be, as to its form, a democratic one as well as a non-democratic one. There are some elections or referenda in which 'the impossible happens' – recall, decades ago in Italy, a referendum on divorce where, to the great surprise also of the Left which distrusted the people, the pro-divorce side convincingly won, so that even the Left, privately sceptical, was ashamed of its distrust. (There were elements of the event even in the unexpected first electoral victory of Mitterrand.) It is only in *such* cases that one is justified in saying that, beyond and above the mere numerical majority, people effectively have spoken in a substantial sense of the term. On the other hand, an authentic act of popular will can also occur in the form of a violent revolution, of a progressive military dictatorship, etc. In this precise sense, Khrushchev's 1956 speech denouncing Stalin's crimes was a true political act – as William Taubman put it, after this speech, 'the Soviet regime never fully recovered, and neither did he'.[2] Although the opportunist motives for this daring move are plain enough, there was clearly more than mere calculation to it, a kind of reckless excess which cannot be accounted for by strategic reasoning. After this speech, things were never the same again, the fundamental dogma of the infallible leadership was undermined, so no wonder that, as a reaction to the speech, the entire nomenklatura sank into temporary paralysis.

So again the question can be asked of whether an authentic act is possible within today's democracy?

Interestingly enough, there is at least one case in which formal democrats themselves (or, at least, a substantial part of them) would tolerate the suspension of democracy: what if the formally free elections are won by an anti-democratic party whose platform promises the abolition of formal democracy? (This did happen, among other places, in Algeria a couple of years ago.) In such a case, many a democrat would concede that the people were not yet 'mature' enough to be allowed democracy, and that some kind of enlightened despotism whose aim will be to educate the majority into proper democrats is preferable. A crucial component of any populism is also the dismissal of the formal democratic procedure: even if these rules are still respected, it is always made clear that they do not provide the crucial legitimacy to political agents – populism rather evokes the direct pathetic link between the charismatic leadership and the crowd, verified through plebiscites and mass gatherings. Consequently, it seems politically much more productive and theoretically much more adequate to limit 'democracy' to the translation of antagonism into agonism: while democracy acknowledges the irreducible plurality of interests, ideologies, narratives, etc., it excludes those who, as we put it, reject the democratic rules of the game – liberal democrats are quite right in claiming that populism is inherently 'anti-democratic'.

This is the sense in which one should render democracy problematic: why should the Left always and unconditionally respect the formal democratic 'rules of the game'? Why should it not, in some circumstances, at least, put in question the legitimacy of the outcome of a formal democratic procedure? All democratic Leftists venerate Rosa Luxemburg's famous 'Freedom is freedom for those who think differently'. Perhaps, the time has come to shift the accent from 'differently' to 'think': 'Freedom is freedom for those who think differently' – *only* for those who *really think*, even if differently, not for those who just blindly (unthinkingly) act out their opinions . . .

In his famous short poem 'The Solution' from 1953 (published in 1956), Brecht mocks the arrogance of the communist nomenklatura for thinking that they could 'dissolve the people' when their opinions did not suit them. However, we would say on the contrary that it effectively *is* a duty – *the* duty even – of a revolutionary party to 'dissolve the people and elect another', i.e., to bring about the transubstantiation of the 'old' opportunistic people (the inert 'crowd') into a revolutionary body aware of its historical task. Far from being an easy task, to 'dissolve the people and elect another' is the most difficult of them all ... What this means is that one should gather the courage radically to question today's predominant attitude of anti-authoritarian tolerance. It was, surprisingly, Bernard Williams who, in his perspicuous reading of David Mamet's *Oleanna*, outlined the limits of this attitude:

> A complaint constantly made by the female character is that she has made sacrifices to come to college, in order to learn something, to be told things that she did not know, but that she has been offered only a feeble permissiveness. She complains that her teacher [...] does not control or direct her enough: he does not tell her what to believe, or even, perhaps, what to ask. He does not exercise authority. At the same time, she complains that he exercises power over her. This might seem to be a muddle on her part, or the playwright's, but it is not. The male character has power over her (he can decide what grade she gets), but just because he lacks authority, this power is mere power, in part gender power.[3]

This takes us back to the question of the modern Master, does it not?

Yes, indeed, power here appears (is experienced) 'as such' at the very point where it is no longer covered by 'authority'. There are, however, further complications to Williams's view. First, 'authority' is not simply a direct property of the Master-figure, but an effect of the social relationship between the Master and his subjects: even if the master remains the same, it may happen, because of the change in the socio-symbolic field, that his position is no longer perceived as legitimate authority but as mere illegitimate power (is such a shift not the most elementary gesture of feminism: male authority is all of a sudden unmasked as mere power?). The lesson of all revolutions from 1789 to 1989 is that such a disintegration of authority, its transformation into arbitrary power, always precedes the revolutionary outbreak. Where Williams is right is in his emphasis on how the very permissiveness of the power-figure, his restraining from exercising authority by directing, controlling, his subject, ensures that his authority appears as illegitimate power. Therein resides the vicious cycle of today's academia: the more professors renounce 'authoritarian' active teaching, imposing knowledge and values, the more they are experienced as figures of power. And, as every parent knows, the same goes for parental education: a father who exerts true transferential authority will never be experienced as 'oppressive' – it is, on the contrary, a father who tries to be permissive, who does not want to impose on his children his views and values, but allows them to discover their own way, who must be denounced as exerting power, as being 'oppressive' . . .

Thank you very much for taking the time to talk with me, Slavoj Žižek.

Notes

Chapter 1: The subject of philosophy

1. There is perhaps only one thing that Žižek will not admit to: looking up his own sales figures on Amazon.com. In a classic example of what he calls 'interpassivity' – enjoyment through the other – he will attribute this to his friends, who then tell him. See on this Christopher Hanlon, 'Psychoanalysis and the Post-Political: An Interview with Slavoj Žižek', *New Literary History* 32 (2001): 7.

2. Or, because anyone who believes anything today runs the risk of being seen as kitsch, we might compare Žižek to another of his literary heroes, the architect Howard Roark from Ayn Rand's *The Fountainhead*:

   Roark stood before them as each man stands in the innocence of his own mind – and they knew suddenly that no hatred was possible to him. For the flash of an instant, they grasped the manner of his consciousness. Each asked himself: do I need anyone's approval? – does it matter? – am I tied? And for that instant, each man was free – free enough to feel benevolence for every other man in the room. (*AF*, 86)

3. Ernesto Laclau and Chantal Mouffe, *Hegemony and Socialist Strategy: Towards a Radical Democratic Politics* (London: Verso, 1985).

4. Cited in Peter Canning, 'The Sublime Theorist of Slovenia', *Artforum* (March 1993): 85.

5. Cited in Guy Mannes Abbott, 'Žižek within the Limits of Mere Reason', *The Independent* (3 May 1999): 42.

6. Cited in Robert S. Boynton, 'Enjoy your Žižek!', *Lingua Franca* 8.7 (October 1998): 48.

7. Edward R. O'Neill, 'The Last Analysis of Slavoj Žižek', *Film-Philosophy* 5.17 (June 2001): 7.

8. As Žižek puts it: 'The only way to produce something real in theory is to pursue the transferential fiction to the end' (*H*, 10). This might be compared to the acquisition of a language: it is only when we have completely internalized it that we can begin to think for ourselves (*ME*, 43–6).

9. Denise Gigante, 'Toward a Notion of Critical Self-Creation: Slavoj Žižek and the "Vortex of Madness" ', *New Literary History* 29 (1998): 453.

10. Some of Žižek's examples of the false 'free' choice that arises after the fundamental 'forced' choice include: that between Nutra-Sweet and High & Low for artificial sweeteners, between Jay Leno and David Letterman for late-night TV, between Coke and Pepsi for beverages (*T?*, 240–41) – and we even might say between the two political parties in most modern democratic duopolies. This is the meaning behind the famous Marx Brothers' joke quoted by Žižek: 'Tea or coffee? Yes, please!' (*CHU*, 240), which operates as a *refusal* of this false choice.

11. As a perfect instance of this, we might think of Cavell's notion of the 'comedy of remarriage', which signifies not so much any actual break-up of the couple as a free repetition of the original 'forced' decision to marry. That is, each of the parties behaves *as though* they were not married and can choose again whether or not to enter into a relationship with the other. See Stanley Cavell, *Pursuits of Happiness: The Hollywood Comedy of Remarriage* (Cambridge, MA: Harvard University Press, 1981).

12. Žižek is perhaps the opposite to Lacan in this regard. He attempts to bring out the 'disparity' between the empty place and what fills it not through his absence but through a kind of over-presence: the split between the mathemic purity of his thought and his physical and emotional 'grossness', his sexist and non-'pc' jokes. His strategy is perhaps not dissimilar to that of contemporary artists, who seek to maintain the sacred 'void' by putting a piece of excrement in its place (*FA*, 30–31).

13. This is also the conclusion Foucault reaches in his essay 'What is an Author?', in which he considers a special class of authors he calls the 'initiators of discursive practices', principally Marx and Freud. In their work, we have not only a 'certain number of analogies that could be adopted by future texts, but they also make possible a number of differences', Michel Foucault, *Language, Counter-Memory, Practice: Selected Essays and Interviews* (Oxford: Basil Blackwell, 1980), p. 132.

Chapter 2: What is a master-signifier?

1. Ernesto Laclau and Chantal Mouffe, *Hegemony and Socialist Strategy: Towards a Radical Democratic Politics* (London: Verso, 1985).

2. As an example of this we might think of George Orwell's novel *1984*. In a first (Imaginary) reading, it is about another, totalitarian country (Russia); but in a second (Symbolic) reading, it is actually about us. It is the liberal, democratic West that is *already* the dystopia Orwell describes; it is *this* world that is seen through *1984*.

3. As for historical instances of this 'paranoia', we might think of the necessity for the Khmer Rouge incessantly to rewrite its origins (*T?*, 97–9) or the infamous spy within the CIA, James Jesus Angleton, whose job was to look for

spies within the CIA (*TK*, xxxvi–vii). This 'paranoia', indeed, is close to that *drive* Žižek wants, in which we always try to find that void or enunciation behind any enunciated; not simply the Other to the Other, but the Other to the Other to the Other … And yet Žižek in the end does not advocate this paranoia, which remains a kind of Hegelian 'bad infinity' in its simple denial of symbolic closure (in this regard, deconstruction is perhaps more like paranoia). Rather, Žižek's challenge is somehow to produce this 'openness' through closure, not to say that the Symbolic is impossible but that the Symbolic *is* its own impossibility (*TK*, 87–8).

4. The point here is that the birds in *The Birds* are precisely not 'symbolic', suggesting different readings of the film, for example, cosmological, ecological, familial (*LA*, 97–8). Rather, the birds as master-signifer allow all of these different readings at once. The birds of *The Birds* would lose their power if they were reduced to any one of these possibilities – and it is part of the effect of the master-signifier that it is able to cover up their radical inconsistency, the fact that they cannot all equally be true (*PF*, 158).

5. In fact, this is why so many movie monsters are already shape-shifting, 'second-degree' creatures, not so much any content in particular as able to move between guises and forms: Howard Hawks' and John Carpenter's *The Thing*, Stephen King's *It*, Woody Allen's *Zelig* (who was also Jewish). All this, as Žižek suggests in his essay on the subject, 'Why Does the Phallus Appear?', is exactly like the *phallus* itself, which is the ultimate 'monster' and what all monsters ultimately resemble (*E!*, 128–9).

6. Undoubtedly, the greatest example of the master-signifier and its accompanying *object a* in literature is to be found in Borges' essay 'Kafka and his Precursors', in which he lists Kafka's various antecedents: 'If I am not mistaken, the heterogeneous pieces I have enumerated resemble Kafka; if I am not mistaken, not all of them resemble each other', Jorges Luis Borges, 'Kafka and his Precursors', in *Labyrinths* (Harmondsworth: Penguin, 1981), p. 236. The first point to understand here is that Kafka is not simply something in common to his various precursors – because they do not all have something in common – but the very *difference* between them. The second point is that Kafka is in fact less 'Kafkaesque' than some of his precursors: 'The early Kafka of *Betrachtung* is less a precursor of the Kafka of sombre myths and atrocious institutions than is Browning or Lord Dunsany' (p. 236). That is, every attempt to say what Kafka is only reduces him to the status of one of his precursors; any attempted metastatement concerning Kafka becomes merely another statement. Here, if Kafka's precursors are 'immediated-abbreviated' by Kafka, and Kafka 'explicates' them, the true 'Kafkaesque' quality Borges is trying to put his finger on is the *relationship* between these: that 'nothing' Kafka and his various precursors have in common. Put simply, 'Kafka' *is* the relationship between Kafka and his precursors.

7. See on this Robert Pfaller's essay 'Negation and its Reliabilities: An Empty Subject for Ideology?' (*CU*, 225–46), which criticizes Žižek's conception of the line 'I am a replicant', from the film *Bladerunner*, as an extra-ideological

statement. Pfaller's point is not that Žižek is simply incorrect but that he does not make that extra turn and ask from where his *own* statement is being stated.

8. *This* is Žižek's point: not that there is no freedom but that *any* expression of freedom is only a distortion of it; that freedom *is* only what allows us to speak of its distortion. And this is the meaning of Žižek saying that the worker is exploited even when he is fully paid (*TS*, 179–80). Here class or class struggle is a kind of 'symptom' that is present in its absence, that is manifest only in its distortion.

Chapter 3: What is an act?

1. To put this another way, both of those other historical approaches claim to be value-free, whereas Benjamin wants a history that explicitly argues for values. In the first, there is no judgement of the past; while, in the second, all judgements are equally possible. In fact, both in subtle ways continue to privilege the present. The 'totality' in the 'location of the interpreted text in the totality of its epoch' (*SO*, 137) is only defined from the point of view of the victors. The apparently free rewriting of history can only take place each time from the 'perspective of the Last Judgement' (*SO*, 142). Or Benjamin does not so much *oppose* this historicism as apply its own logic to it. As Žižek in *Contingency, Hegemony, Universality* (*CHU*, 106–7), he *historicizes historicism*, asks what is excluded to make it possible.

2. It is in this sense that Deleuze is able to say, through Bergson, that every present brings out a different past 'in itself', a past that never was. See on this Gilles Deleuze, *Cinema II: The Time-Image* (London: The Athlone Press, 1989), pp. 80, 294.

3. It is the idea that this 'revolutionary potential' exists only as its loss that is that 'second death' Žižek speaks of in *Sublime Object* (*SO*, 144–5). It is this very 'revolutionary potential' that ensures that nothing is outside of history (as opposed to historicism, which is always 'in between' deaths in preserving some point outside of history). As Benjamin writes: '*Even the dead* will not be safe from the enemy if he wins' (*SO*, 144).

4. This 'rotary cycle' is like that paranoid logic we looked at in Chapter 2, in which the system is never able to move on but must always keep on starting again (the endless purges of Stalinism, the Khmer Rouge beginning at year zero). This 'paranoid' failure, that of an absence unable to click over into presence, is the other side as it were of the Stalinist 'perversion' of thinking that our Cause or history already exists without us, of a presence without absence (*PF*, 222).

5. As Žižek says, Schelling breaks with the 'fantasy' of the act as a kind of temporal loop by which God gives rise to Himself, as though 'prior to this beginning the subject is miraculously present as a pure gaze observing His own non-existence' (*IR*, 19). This could be compared to Žižek's very similar analysis of the fantasy of the 'primal scene' in *For They Know Not* (*TK*, 197–8).

6. This is more complicated than it appears. Žižek will choose one example in order to prove that he cannot choose one example (both that there is no exception or example within capitalism and that this example is not fundamentally what he is speaking about, is always to miss it). And yet at the same time within the 'sinthomic' not-all of capitalism there are *only* exceptions or examples (and this is the way Žižek's own work is increasingly structured, as almost an endless series of examples with no linking argument). It is this that complexifies Diane Chisholm's otherwise excellent 'Žižek's Exemplary Culture', *Journal for the Psychoanalysis of Culture and Society* 6.2 (Fall 2001).

7. For example, Žižek several times in his work notes the self-contradiction of Badiou's directly anti-statist politics: that it needs a state to argue against (*TK*, lxxxii–iii; *TS*, 170). This is exactly that cycle betweeen the law and its transgression that St Paul sought to overcome. And this would be why Badiou's politics – for all of their opposition to Kant – ultimately take the form of the Kantian 'infinite ethical effort' (*TS*, 166; *B*, 125).

8. The death-drive makes of everything a failure in its continued inability to be thought. However, as with 'antagonism' in our previous chapter, we do not actually see this failure; this death-drive is not some identitifiable tic or symptom that is repeated. This is the conventional misunderstanding of psychoanalysis. Rather, the death-drive makes of every apparent 'success' a failure, of whatever we do a repetition. It is in this sense that it is not simply some void *before* things for which they stand in, but things themselves *as their own absence*, that 'Cause' that exists when there is no Cause.

Chapter 4: The 'negation of negation'

1. See on this Žižek's insistence that today it is 'more important than ever to hold this utopian place of the global alternative open' (*CHU*, 325). And it is this that underlies the distinction Žižek frequently makes between Nazism and communism (*TS*, 138–9; *CHU*, 124–5). Although both of these might appear to constitute 'acts', it is Nazism with its attempt to go 'all the way' that works only to keep things the same, while it is communism, in maintaining the 'fundamental choice', that actually changes things. This is also Žižek's criticism of the 11 September hijackings: that they immediately undergo the *passage à l'acte* only to avoid the true decision (*DR!*, 11–12).

2. This could undoubtedly be related to us here, in so far as we read Žižek against himself, hold him up to standards that he himself sets (an attitude that, as we have said, ensures that any criticisms we make of Žižek will always return to Žižek himself, that he will always be seen to be responding to them in advance). So why are we not like this? Perhaps because we also try to think here that Žižek is *not* all that we say before we say it, that there is something that cannot be reduced to this circular mode of analysis. This again would be the 'split subject' of philosophy that would think the sacrifice or giving up of the Cause (as Cause).

3. That is, there is no final 'perspective of the Last Judgement' in the post-totalitarian world, as Benjamin so presciently foresaw (*SO*, 144). There is rather an
incessant series of judgements and revisions without end. Hence the terrifying
anecdote Žižek relates of the Yugoslavian communists who returned from the
death camps after the Second World War and, instead of being greeted as
heroes – in that Symbolic immortality granted by risking biological death –
were immediately tried for treason by the new government (*L*, 272).

4. Without getting into the much contested distinction between Radical and
Diabolical Evil (*PF*, 226–30), we might say that Diabolical Evil is the idea
that the Good arises only as an effect of our positing; but that we are in this
not acting *for* the Good because the Good does not yet exist. It is the Good
undertaken for the 'wrong', that is, not Good, reasons – an impossibility for
Kant, but necessary for his moral system to be constituted.

5. In Cavell's essay on the film, 'Stella's Taste', he also makes the point that it is
not in this a matter of some exception, of some eternal feminine 'irony of the
community'. Rather, if he speaks of Stella as 'unknown', she is unknown not
merely to the various men in her life but also *to herself*. That is, it is a question
here also, as with Copjec's 'love', of thinking what is lost by the subject's entry
into the Symbolic. See on this Stanley Cavell, *Contesting Tears: The Hollywood
Melodrama of the Unknown Woman* (Cambridge, MA: Harvard University
Press, 1990), pp. 200–1.

6. Robert S. Boynton, 'Enjoy Your Žižek!', *Lingua Franca* 8.7 (October 1998): 50

7. It is tempting, for example, to see the last chapters of many of Žižek's books
as a mere 'application' of his theory, apparently tacked on at the end. In fact,
we might understand their seemingly 'practical' suggestions as purely 'formal': as a kind of 'Real' that, in its impossibility, marks what is as a failure.
We return to this in our Conclusion; but it is hinted at as a strategy as long
ago as *Enjoy Your Symptom!*, in which Žižek says of Adorno's similar 'vulgar-
sociological references' that they:

> Prevent the thought from falling into the trap of identity and mistaking the
> limited form of reflection for the unattainable form of thought as such.
> In other words, the function of the 'vulgar-sociological' reference is to
> represent within the notional *content* what eludes notion as such, namely the
> totality of its own *form*. (*E!*, 85)

8. See on this Zupančič's important comments on the post-tragic state of
Claudel's heroine Sygne de Coûfontaine, who despite knowing that she is
going to fail nevertheless for this very reason goes ahead and completes her
actions: 'We can see in Sygne de Coûfontaine an Oedipus who knows ...
[who is unable] to escape the calamity of her acts thanks to her knowledge
but, rather, finds herself in a situation where this very knowledge compels
her to take the decision to commit them' (*ER*, 256). Žižek for his part says of
Sygne that her actions can at once be read as the 'lowest cynicism ("I know
what I am about to do is the lowest depravity, but what the hell, who cares,
I'll just do it ...")' and the 'highest tragic split ("I am fully aware of the

catastrophic consequences of what I am about to do, but I can't help it, it's my unconditional duty to do it, so I'll go on with it")' (*TS*, 387). And it is precisely this duality that we see in Žižek himself: as many commentators have noted, there is a disturbing mixture in him of the utterly sincere and the entirely ironic; proposing sweeping philosophical and political insights, but, if pushed, rapidly disclaiming them, turning them into a joke, mocking his audience for taking them seriously.

Chapter 5: Žižek on others: others on Žižek

1. See Judith Butler, 'Arguing with the Real', in *Bodies that Matter* (London and New York: Routledge, 1993).
2. See on this debate Barbara Johnson's 'The Frame of Reference: Poe, Lacan, Derrida', *Yale French Studies* 55/56 (1977).
3. Intriguingly, Žižek's attempt to think the simultaneity of the empirical and the transcendental can be compared to a similar attempt to do so by the deconstructionist Geoffrey Bennington. As Bennington writes in his essay 'X' (the same 'X', we would suggest, that Žižek discusses in the chapter 'The Deadlock of Transcendental Imagination' in *Ticklish Subject*): 'X is mysterious and possibly forbidden: the two lines [of the transcendental and the empirical] define a pure, vanishing point. This point is the point of transcendentality itself, in its endless collapse into the empirical', in *Interrupting Derrida* (London: Routledge, 2000), p. 83.
4. See Peter Dews, 'The Tremor of Reflection: Slavoj Žižek's Lacanian Dialectics', *Radical Philosophy* 72 (July–August, 1995): 25–6, and 'The Eclipse of Coincidence: Lacan, Merleau-Ponty and Schelling', *Angelaki* 4.3 (1999): 22.
5. And on this whole strategy of introducing a kind of 'split' or 'undecidability' into what is by means of these purely 'formal' statements, who would say that Žižek is wrong here? Who would bet that the fate of the West and capitalism is truly assured? Which way will the current occupation of Iraq go? What will be the outcome of the ongoing 'war against Terror'? When will the increasing scarcity of the world's resources finally begin to tell against us? And has not this 'undecidability' always been the case? Has not human civilization always confronted the 'same' absolute ambiguity, although in always different forms?

Chapter 6: Žižek live

1. See Eric Santner, *My Own Private Germany* (Princeton, NJ: Princeton University Press, 1996).
2. William Taubman, *Khrushchev: The Man and His Era* (London: Free Press, 2003) p. 493.
3. Bernard Williams, *Truth and Truthfulness* (Princeton, NJ: Princeton University Press, 2002) pp. 7–8.

Index

Index of names